Contents

	Preface	*page* 6
1	The Organisational Perspective	7
2	The Goals of the British Educational System	10
3	The Overall Structure of British Education	23
4	The Role of the Head	38
5	The Role of the Teacher	52
6	The School	67
7	The School Class	85
	Postscript	97
	Bibliography	98
	Glossary	100
	Index	102

Preface

Several sociologists have commented that my earlier book, *The Sociology of Education*, contained no serious consideration of educational institutions from the standpoint of organisation theory. I am, therefore, very grateful to Professor and Mrs O'Connor for asking me to write a book in this series and allowing me to try to put right something of my earlier omission. I also wish to thank two of my colleagues in the Department of Sociology in the University of Aberdeen – Alan Davis for much help and constructive criticism, and Tony Wootton for some comments on the Glossary. Naturally, the final responsibility for this book is mine.

Aberdeen, 1968 P. W. M.

BASIC BOOKS IN EDUCATION

Editor: *Kathleen O'Connor, B.Sc., Senior Lecturer in Education, Rolle College, Exmouth*
Advisory Editor: *D. J. O'Connor, M.A., Ph.D., Professor of Philosophy, University of Exeter*

The School as an Organisation

Dr Musgrave's new book presents a simple comparative analysis of the English and Scottish school system in the framework of modern sociological organisation theory. It begins with an historical analysis of the main goals of education in England and Scotland and leads on to a description of the roles of the headteacher and class teacher. Finally, the organisation of the school as a whole and of the school class is analysed.

Key words in the text are in SMALL CAPITALS, there are summaries and 'further reading' lists at the end of each chapter, and there is a full bibliography, glossary and index.

The School as an Organisation

P. W. MUSGRAVE, M.A., Ph.D.

SENIOR LECTURER IN SOCIOLOGY

UNIVERSITY OF ABERDEEN

MACMILLAN

London · Melbourne · Toronto

1968

Published by
MACMILLAN AND CO LTD
Little Essex Street London WC 2
and also at Bombay Calcutta and Madras
Macmillan South Africa (Publishers) Pty Ltd Johannesburg
The Macmillan Company of Australia Pty Ltd Melbourne
The Macmillan Company of Canada Ltd Toronto

Printed in Great Britain by
ROBERT MACLEHOSE AND CO LTD
The University Press, Glasgow

1 The Organisational Perspective

In the last ten years a theory of organisations has become an established part of the field of sociology. In this context an ORGANISATION is defined as a system of co-ordinated activity carried out by two or more persons for a definite purpose. Sociologists have tended to concentrate on complex organisations. One important category of organisation is exemplified by the factory. In this case the efficiency of the organisation in reaching its goal, namely the long-term maximisation of profit, can usually be measured fairly easily. There is another category that is of increasing importance in contemporary Britain, namely service organisations such as hospitals. In this case efficiency in reaching the goal given to the organisation is much harder to estimate. The purpose of this book is to examine in some detail the present state of knowledge about one important service organisation, the school. This aim will have been achieved if, as a result, readers are better able to teach in schools because they have a greater awareness of both the external forces and of the internal processes that affect schools.

For an organisation to reach its goal co-ordination is essential and therefore to anyone analysing organisations a major emphasis must be on the problem of who has POWER and how it is used. Under contemporary conditions a very common mode of co-ordinating activity and regulating power is to establish a BUREAUCRACY. For sociologists this term has a definite meaning. It refers to a hierarchy of POSITIONS each of which is governed by known rules and to which incumbents are recruited in a more or less regulated way. By this very rational method the organisation is enabled to continue for the purpose for which it was set up despite changes in its personnel. The school goes on and children are taught though there is a new head and though many staff are new.

We have defined organisational activity as purposeful. For this reason the first task in this book will be to specify the goals of contemporary education (see chapter 2). The goals of organisations that have existed for some time tend to be much affected by their past. This is especially true in Britain where evolutionary change has been the rule for the last two centuries. It is particularly the case for schools since they are not so directly in touch with the forces of social change as are, for example, economic organisations. The goals of the latter change with their profit and loss account while the goals of schools tend to lag behind social needs. It is for these reasons that the historical residues still working on the contemporary educational system must be discovered in any study of the goals of schools. When any society has effectively defined the goals of such an institution as education it will ensure that resources are channelled into building a system to carry out these aims. Therefore we must look at the overall structure of the educational system (chapter 3). This forms a major part of the environment within which individual schools exist and also acts as a constraint upon the way any school interacts with other organisations or institutions.

Once schools are set up positions for staff are established within them. The bigger the school the more complex will be its structure and the more bureaucratic its nature. Its hierarchy will include the positions of head, deputy head, perhaps several departmental heads, and many teachers. For each of these different positions there will be more or less defined expectations of behaviour. Therefore the next step will be to examine the ROLE of the head (chapter 4) and the role of the teacher (chapter 5). Again, and for the same reasons as when examining goals a historical perspective will be necessary.

Organisations are established to meet one or more particular purposes, but time and again sociologists have found that they may be hindered or even directed towards new goals by internal processes. It seems a sociological rule that organisations come to lead something of a life of their own, independent of their stated purposes. In any analysis of the working of such a complex organisation as a school the nature of these important internal processes must be discerned. Only in this way is it possible to counteract forces that may divert the school from achieving its goals. Very important influences are both the clients of the organisation – the customers of a shop or the pupils in a school – and the staff recruited to man the organisation – the shop assistants or the teachers. So, finally, the processes within the school (chapter 6) and the processes within the classroom (chapter 7) will be examined.

Throughout this book footnotes have been kept to a minimum. As yet, there is not a large British literature specifically dealing with schools as organisations. However, at the end of each chapter there is a brief list of the more important work to which reference may be made for further reading. In all chapters except the first, the reader is referred at the relevant point in the text to these works by citing the author's name and the number of the book or article concerned in the bibliography at the end of this book. The meaning of technical terms is made clear on the occasion that they are first used, but there is a glossary at the end of the book. The relevant words are printed in bold type.

FURTHER READING

Ashley, Cohen and Slatter (1). A companion volume in this series, contains definitions of the main sociological terms used in this and other chapters.

Bidwell (5). A very full account of the American literature together with a bibliography.

Hoyle (33). A good introduction to organisation theory as applied to schools with references to some British work.

2 The Goals of the British Educational System

In this chapter a brief account will be given of the way in which the contemporary goals of the British educational system have developed. Four areas are of major importance. These are: goals connected with religion; the cluster of related goals concerned with the struggle to move from an élitist to a more egalitarian social system; goals connected with the economy; and the degree of independence to be allowed to the schools.

This chapter has been entitled 'The Goals of the *British* Educational System'. Most writers on education deal with either the English or the Scottish schools. Individual comparisons of detail are rarely made and almost never are the two systems considered on a comparative basis (Osborne, 25). Therefore an essential part of the argument of this chapter is a justification of the position taken. Briefly, the hypothesis is that in these four important areas the goals of English and Scottish schools are much the same today, though this position has been reached by very different paths. Indeed, the present similarity of goals could, at least theoretically, be no more than a temporary situation, a crossing point as the educational systems of the two nations develop along their separate ways into the future.

RELIGION

There has been more difference between England and Scotland here than in the other three goal areas. After the English Reformation the Church of England rigidly controlled the right to teach. Only those who had been given a licence signed by a bishop were allowed to act as schoolmasters. The Church enforced this policy because of the belief that control of education led to control of people's minds. Throughout the seventeenth century, as the Dissenting churches grew in strength, the established Church of England fought a losing battle to maintain this licensing system.

By the eighteenth century it had become clear that Dissent was to be a permanent force in the land and the Church gradually evolved a new policy on education. This was based on the assumption that the education of the masses was of more importance for the future of the Church than that of the élite. The schools for the poor became part of the missionary field. Education was seen as an outlet for the charity of the wealthy, a socially acceptable means of achieving grace. The aim was that the poor were to be rescued from ignorance through being taught the faith of the Church and, in addition, since the Church was the established one, they were to be taught their God-given status in society. Naturally the various non-conformist sects took up a somewhat similar position if only in their own defence. Thus the English school for the lower classes came to be run by religious bodies in a missionary spirit.

When the demand came in the nineteenth century for a national system and for some form of state aid, the religious denominations were in a position of strength since they were the main providers of schools at that time. So in a laissez-faire age each of the various denominations competed with the others to bring the poor into their own fold of true believers through the instrument of their schools. They all opposed the introduction of state aid which seemed to them to be no more than a subsidy to their competitors. In 1870 a compromise was reached so that the Elementary Education Act was passed for England. As a result of this Act a new system of schools provided by the state was established alongside the existing schools provided by the denominations. The religious goals of education were so important at the time that the problem of much wider provision could only be solved by the creation of a dual system.

As the English educational system was expanded by successive Acts of Parliament in 1902 and 1944 the resulting organisational framework has retained the marks of the compromise made in 1870. A large proportion of English schools are still provided by denominations, mainly by the Church of England, or by the Roman Catholic Church, and hence religious goals are much more to the fore in these schools than in schools provided by the state. Yet, because of this long history of religious difficulty, the Education Act of 1944 which is still in operation today may be described as a Christian Act. It largely preserves the dual system in England and Wales and ensures that some priority is given to religious instruction even in provided schools.

In Scotland John Knox published his *First Book of Discipline* in 1560. From this work may be dated the start of the system of Scottish parochial schools. The established Church of Scotland from its earliest days rated education as a high priority among its goals. As a result, by the eighteenth century Scotland could be said to have had a national educational system based on the parishes of the Presbyterian church. In addition, there were a small number of schools run by other denominations, mainly the Church of England and the Roman Catholic Church, but unlike the situation south of the border there was no real religious difficulty over education. Primarily this can be attributed to the moral and numerical predominance of the Presbyterians who felt no threat from other denominations.

After the 1830s government grants were made to denominational schools in England and Scotland for certain purposes under the control of codes drawn up in London, but little difference was made to the positions of the religious bodies except to strengthen their claims as sole providers of education for the poor in England and the nation in Scotland. Following the English Education Act of 1870 an Act was passed for Scotland in 1872, but, since there was no religious problem in Scotland, this Act provided that religious instruction should continue as before in the schools. Denominational schools could opt to be taken over by the newly established School Boards with complete protection of their rights to teach denominational religious instruction. By the next major Scottish Education Act, that of 1918, denominational schools had to opt to be taken over by the Local Education Authorities or lose their government grants. Thus, when the 1945 Education Act extended to Scotland the principles of the 1944 English Act, there was no religious problem or dual system, though there was a strong tradition, dating back to John Knox, of seeing the schools as having religious goals.

In the past religious bodies have played a predominant part in the provision of education in both England and Scotland because they believed that education had a fundamentally religious goal. Yet the religious history of England and Scotland has been different. Thus, though religious instruction is still seen as central to the ethos and the curriculum of the schools of both countries, it is only in England that the actual organisational framework has been deeply affected by the religious structure of the past.

ELITISM VERSUS EGALITARIANISM

The political forces working towards greater egalitarianism in the last century and a half have been common to England and Scotland, though they have worked on societies originally determined by very different histories. At the start of the nineteenth century England was basically an aristocratic country with an underdeveloped educational system that catered almost entirely for the élite (Musgrave, 24). Certainly the two English universities of Oxford and Cambridge for the most part served an aristocratic clientele. Scotland was more democratic. The son of the laird and his shepherd went together to the parochial school, and the more developed educational system was viewed by most Scots as the main pathway for moving up in social class. The Scottish parochial school, largely financed out of parish monies, was a way to one of the four university cities for the 'lad o' pairts', even though he lacked great means. In Scotland the professional élite, particularly the lawyers, the ministers and the schoolteachers, were to a considerable extent recruited from the lower classes through this educational route.

As a result of the reform of parliament in 1832 the middle class came nearer to political power. During the succeeding decades the large number of sinecures that had existed were abolished so that no longer were the sons of the élite guaranteed places of power in the government and in the expanding civil service. Entry to such positions came to be controlled by the somewhat fairer means of examinations. Furthermore, new universities were established in England and from their foundation these were seen, as was the case in Scotland, to have a direct link with the professional and industrial middle classes. Because of these changes the middle class in England, as in Scotland, came to realise that it needed secondary education. In a laissez-faire situation there was a demand for more secondary school places. In the case of the expanding upper middle class, secondary education was also wanted to ensure for its children the new STATUS that it claimed because of its new wealth. Thus there was an increasing demand for the old élite-type education provided by the public schools. By the last third of the century a similar demand resulted in the establishment of a small number of public schools even in Scotland.

One result of the nature of this demand for secondary education was that the old classical curriculum was seen as what should be taught despite the needs, more frequently recognised as the century progressed, for school subjects that would be of more direct use to an industrial nation. A knowledge of the classical and humane curriculum, inherited from the medieval grammar school, was thought to be the mark of an educated man of the leisured class and hence was seen as what should be taught to the son of a man aspiring to higher status. In turn, the new proprietary day secondary schools were influenced to teach much the same curriculum, though many of these schools did provide some science and mathematics in answer to local needs. In Scotland, the classical curriculum had always retained its vocational significance as a requirement for those going from the elementary school through university to the various traditional professions.

The second reform of parliament in 1867 in its turn allowed the working class to approach political power. Before long, it was demanding an easier entry to secondary education. In England, the need was defined as the creation of the sort of scholarship ladder that already existed in Scotland. In this latter country, the new demands for a more egalitarian society meant the extension of the existing system. In both countries, the forces at work to retain the classical curriculum influenced what was taught in the new state-provided elementary schools. In England those who had already made their way up the social scale, for example teachers and higher grade clerks, had made their way by learning the 3 Rs, not science or handwork. In Scotland, the view already mentioned that a classical type curriculum had vocational significance prevailed. In these circumstances, the curriculum changed little despite the move towards a greater degree of educational egalitarianism.

In both countries this process was speeded by the war of 1914–18 and the growing power of labour as a political force. Emancipation of women extended formal secondary education to girls. In addition, there were important technical developments in the field of psychology, more particularly in mental testing and measurement, in which the Scottish universities played a prominent part. These improvements seemed to imply greater fairness in the allocation of children to the scarce free or assisted places in secondary schools. The new psychological theories also appeared to justify the pattern of historical development of the educational system. The elementary schools and the secondary schools had grown apart and even in the more democratic Scottish system it was from the secondary schools that pupils progressed to higher education. The secondary school was for those who were intellectually able; the elementary school was for those who were less able. In addition, especially in England, a third type of school had developed, the technical school which catered for those who seemed to be more gifted with their hands than with their minds and in the 1930s a test was developed which measured even this factor.

In the inter-war years and during the period up to the 1944 Act (1945 for Scotland) the growing demand for 'Secondary Education for All' was interpreted as a call for a tripartite system developed from the existing three types of school, but with parity of esteem given to each type (Banks, 2). After the end of the 1939–45 war the development of the educational system that followed the passing of the 1944 Act was based on this definition of equality. Yet criticisms of this interpretation that were rooted in a more egalitarian spirit grew more common. There were demands for a comprehensive secondary system and for the abolition of both the élitist grammar school and the new modern secondary school that had taken over the education of the older age range of the former elementary school. These new demands were fundamentally political in nature, rather than educational, being based on egalitarian principles, but they received much support from the post-war work of sociologists who, during the 1950s, showed very clearly the extremely unequal chances that the various social classes had of reaching grammar school or university. This work also indicated that much of the so-called innate ability that psychological tests had been thought to measure was really a result of the varied experiences that children of different social classes underwent, particularly during their upbringing at home. By the 1960s criticism of the tripartite system and of the continued existence of the public schools became strong and well-founded on respectable research findings.

In both England and Scotland the demand for a more egalitarian educational system has been strong throughout the last hundred years. This demand has been most easily met in Scotland. In both countries, however, the evolutionary pattern of development has ensured that much that remains from the past has hindered a rapid achievement of the new goal of greater egalitarianism that has been given to the educational system. In one particular respect, namely the content of the curriculum, the forces of egalitarianism have worked to preserve the prevailing curriculum despite the strong case on economic grounds that changes should be made.

ECONOMIC GOALS

Since the mid-eighteenth century, the process of industrialisation has been at work in Britain – a society permeated by the ideal of laissez-faire. In both England and Scotland, much the same economic forces have had very similar effects. During the first century of this industrial revolution the level of technology was such that there was no big demand for a formally educated labour force. Hence, under the laissez-faire conditions ruling, no educational machinery was brought into being to supply educated manpower. This was the age of the self-taught man

(Hans, 15). In Scotland Adam Smith in his *Wealth of Nations* (1776) admitted the existence of a link between education and economic well-being that might need nurturing by the state. Yet despite the traditional priority given to education there was no general realisation, even in Scotland, that more schools might be needed to meet the latent needs of a labour force that was coming to rely more on scientific knowledge.

Only after the process of industrialisation had been at work for about a century did the educational shortcomings of the labour force at every level, from manager down to workman, become more obvious. A symbolic occasion was the Great Exhibition of 1851. Here the challenge from foreign competition to Britain's industrial primacy was clear for all to see, as was the increasing complexity and scientific nature of industry. Facilities had to be created at every level and over the next fifty or so years the government either provided or assisted the provision of education at elementary, secondary and higher levels.

But the contemporary economic and political ideologies defined the nature of state aid. Thus the laissez-faire business IDEOLOGY of the time, together with the still powerful élitist idea that education should fit the different levels of society according to their status, governed the way the schools developed. For the mass of people, all that was thought necessary was an elementary education which may briefly be described as a minimal and cheap version of the 3 Rs. Education was run on strictly businesslike lines and grants to individual schools, which in turn determined the salaries of teachers, were governed by a system of payment by results. This spirit also came to rule in Scotland since economic development there necessitated the same expansion of the schools as in England and state aid was given from the central Treasury in London under similar regulations to those governing in England.

The low status and the ethos of cheapness with which the state provision of education was associated in these early days still tends to cling to some types of British schools. Nor must it be forgotten that much of the new secondary provision of the late nineteenth century was called into being to answer the demands of the now wealthier and more numerous middle-class parents.

Such proprietary schools had to be economically viable like any other business. As has been indicated, the paradoxical nature of the demand ensured that the new secondary schools survived largely by supplying a classical curriculum.

In the twentieth century, especially since the end of the second world war, economic goals have pressed hard on both the quantity and the quality of educational provision. There has been an increasing need to see the serving of the labour force as one of the main goals of the schools (Musgrave, 23). This was particularly true of the demand to increase the number of places in selective secondary schools with the aim of tapping the nation's pool of capability to the maximum. The new salience that was given to the economic goals of the schools worked to reinforce the pressure for a more egalitarian system that has already been described.

Simultaneously, there was a switch away from the old stress on a classical and humanist curriculum towards a greater emphasis on science. The teaching of mathematics and of those pure sciences of most value to industry was given more prominence in the schools. The same influences were at work in higher education and new universities of a purely technological nature have recently been developed in both England and Scotland. This is a more revolutionary change in the Scottish than the English idea of a university; in the four ancient Scottish universities priority is still given to the goal of providing a general education through the Ordinary degree.

Under these economic forces the aims of education have undergone a subtle change. Academic excellence in Britain in the middle of the nineteenth century had as its main goal the intellectual development of the individual, although it was realised that educational success was very often instrumental in occupational success. By the mid-twentieth century the social function of education, especially *vis-à-vis* the economy, has come to be paramount and often the development of the individual is put second. In brief, the needs of the economy have influenced the scale and nature of educational provision but, in addition, the economic ideology of laissez-faire predominated in a rather extreme form during the period when the educational system in its present form came into being. This has left a residue that still influences the way in which educational goals are implemented.

INDEPENDENCE

In comparison with the educational systems of many other countries those of England and Scotland have as a goal that individual schools be given considerable scope for independence. The degree of independence permitted differs in the two countries. It is probably somewhat greater in England than in Scotland and the way by which the present situation has been reached is not identical.

The roots of the considerable freedom given to English schools today can be traced to the development of secondary schools in the nineteenth century. Once again the ideology of laissez-faire was important. The new proprietary schools were seen as profit-making enterprises run by a special type of entrepreneur, the headmaster. In industry the head of a business had absolute responsibility; the risks he ran brought him his profit (or loss). This economic reasoning was extended to the schools as educational enterprises. This same right of independence could easily be claimed by the older endowed schools, many of which became public schools as their fee-paying pupils came to be more numerous than their scholarship pupils. The nineteenth-century headmaster in a secondary school successfully claimed great freedom to run his organisation in his own way as long as he met the needs of those paying for his services.

In the elementary schools independence was not always so certain. At the start of the nineteenth century, where they existed these schools possessed a freedom based on the fact that they were, in the main, commercial units whose teacher had to ensure profitability, either by meeting the rather uncritical needs of clients or by following the policies of those who, often out of charity, supplied subsidies. After the 1830s some state aid became available to such schools in an endeavour to lay the foundations of an elementary system. The price of such aid was the forfeiting of much freedom. Inspectors were appointed to see that the code of regulations by which money was granted was obeyed. However, in the Education Acts of 1870 for England and 1872 for Scotland a political force worked for the freedom of the elementary schools. There was a feeling that local democracy should directly influence the provision of schools in any area. By creating locally elected School Boards, local needs could be met as well as the demands of the central government for a businesslike efficiency in the spending of state money. Local education was to be to some extent free of central dictate.

As a result of the 1902 Education Act for England it became possible for local authorities to provide grammar schools. Steps were taken to see that these schools should develop in the same way as their forbears, the private secondary schools. Each school was given a board of governors as a buffer between itself and higher authority. The headmaster was seen as an independent figure of power just as he was in a public school. By the 1944 Act the new primary schools in England were given a similar system: each was to have a Board of Managers. Partly, this development can be attributed to the fact that denominational elementary schools, many of which catered for all ages of pupils, usually had local arrangements for self-government, such as a committee of trustees. When these schools entered the state system more fully as primary schools, catering only for the younger age ranges, the continuance was seen as necessary to guard the interests of the religious denomination concerned. But this goal of religious freedom fitted easily with the goal of overall independence for all schools and so there was no ideological objection to extending the system of governors to all the new primary schools.

In Scotland the situation is somewhat different. Since there had never been a dual system, such committees, though they had existed in some schools in the inter-war years, had not the same purpose and were therefore not built into the 1945 Act and the subsequent reorganisation of the Scottish educational system. Local authorities have independence *vis-à-vis* the central authority, but governing bodies do not exist. Yet the Scottish head has considerable freedom of action based on two historic forces. The traditional high status of the dominie as a professional man has protected the independence of the head and of his school from excessive interference from the Scottish Education Department (SED), though there was a period in the first quarter of this century when the SED tried to impose a great degree of central control from Edinburgh. Secondly, the great popular respect given to education has protected the school, perhaps in an excessively conservative way, from the criticisms of its clients, or rather from their parents.

Thus in both countries the educational systems have been given independence at the local level to develop in great measure as they feel right. This freedom has been passed on to heads and hence to schools, especially at the secondary level, and perhaps to a rather greater degree in England than in Scotland.

SUMMARY

The argument of this chapter is that four goal areas have been of continuous importance in the growth of British education though in a somewhat different way in England and in Scotland. In the evolutionary setting that has existed in these two countries, the form that these goals take today has been much influenced by the path through which the educational system has reached its present state of development. Despite the decline in religion as a major social force religious goals are influential in the present structure of the system, in the curriculum of the schools and, as will be seen subsequently, in the role given to the headmaster. Egalitarianism is hindered by the remnants of the élitist tripartite organisation. Economic goals are more to the fore in the structure of the curriculum, though the classical spirit of the old grammar schools, whether rightly or wrongly, checks the move towards a true scientific education. Again, the aim of business efficiency in education, a field where the calculus of profit and loss is hard to apply, is particularly salient, especially in those types of school with historically low status. Finally, independence remains a strong tradition in British education and this goal carries the rider that the first three goals must somehow be thoroughly instilled in teachers and administrators. If this is not achieved, the present pattern of British education will not be maintained, since independence implies the possibility of change. In the rest of this book the contemporary organisation of the structure of British education and of British schools will be analysed in the light of these four goal areas and of their historical development.

FURTHER READING

Banks (2). An analysis of the way in which the changing definition of the goal of egalitarianism has led to different administrative arrangements for schools during the period from 1900 to 1950.

Cruickshank (9). A historical account of the changing educational goals of religious bodies in England since 1800 and their influence on educational provision.

Hans (15). A historical account of the way in which private schools of various types were called into being mainly by economic needs in the eighteenth century so that ultimately the self-taught man became relatively less common.

Lester Smith (19). In this introductory text chapter 4, 'Economic and Social Factors', chapter 7, 'Some Important Influences' (mainly religious) and chapter 8, 'Education and Industry', are relevant and each has a full bibliography.

Musgrave (23). Chapter I, 'Change, the Labour Force and Education' is an account of the way in which the educational system links with the economy. The rest of this book traces the way this relationship has altered in Britain and Germany since 1860.

Musgrave (24). One strand in this brief sociological analysis of English educational history is the move from an élitist to an egalitarian system.

Osborne (25). This pioneer work compares English and Scottish education. The stress is on administrative rather than sociological issues, though the way goals are translated into institutions is central.

3 The Overall Structure of British Education

Once the members of a society have come to an agreement, whether by a conscious process or merely through unconscious acceptance, on the goals for education a more or less exact definition becomes possible of the way in which these goals will be translated into administrative machinery. Such a definition may be incorporated in legislation or regulations or may merely be an unquestioned assumption. As a result, finance can be allocated to create or to sustain educational institutions. Here the overall structure of the contemporary British educational system will be examined in the light of the four goal areas isolated in the last chapter. This administrative framework forms an important part of the environment within which the schools exist as formal organisations.

THE ADMINISTRATIVE FRAMEWORK

The Treasury is responsible for the expenditure of the government and turns priorities into allocations of finance with which resources of manpower and materials can be claimed. To a great extent the priority of any form of expenditure may be judged by the proportion of the gross national product (GNP) that is spent upon it. The share given to education has been rising in recent years. Between 1954–5 and 1964–5 the share of GNP that went to education rose from 3.2% to 5.1%.

In a sense, the Treasury works to translate the goals of the nation into monetary terms. Thus the fact that in 1964–5 about 25% of educational expenditure went on primary education, 34% on secondary education and 13% on the universities reflects the expansion of secondary and higher education which in turn may be traced to the great stress put upon egalitarianism and upon the educational needs of the economy. However, as well as interpreting the overall priorities that the nation has decided through the democratic process the Treasury can have some say in determining the allocation between sectors within individual spheres of expenditure. It is possible for policy to be born autonomously within the Treasury.

The Department of Education and Science

Once any sector of government becomes particularly complex it tends to be hived off and detailed administration is delegated to a department. In Britain, the task of administering and coordinating the educational system is the responsibility of the Department of Education and Science (DES); in Scotland the Scottish Education Department has a large measure of freedom in interpreting the overall goals of British education within the Scottish tradition. In any such administrative organisation the positions and roles available are governed by the goals given and by the NORMS of those recruited to fill these positions. One of the peculiarities of the educational system is that these norms are in large part learnt within the system itself. This is a conservative influence since those who grow up within the normative climate of the system go back into it holding the views they learnt there.

The pattern of historical growth of any organisation is another major determinant of the nature of the positions and roles available within it. During the nineteenth century, when the British educational system was developing, the power of the ideology of business has been shown to have had a great influence. The budget became the main instrument for controlling state spending. In every sector both capital and current expenditure had to be specified in great detail. This was as true of a service sector such as education as it was of a state enterprise such as the Post Office. A check was built into the system so that the government, on behalf of the nation, was sure that educational expenditure was spent on the purposes for which it was voted. Inspectors were appointed with the aim of seeing that the schools used state money only in accordance with the regulations by which it was granted.

However, the source of recruitment of these HMIs (Her Majesty's Inspectors) was very important during the formative period of the British educational system. There was only one type of man available who could efficiently fill these positions and the same was true in the case of the civil servants who were recruited to fill the administrative positions in the growing Education Department. The level of education needed was such that graduates were essential and in the middle of the nineteenth century in England the main source of such educated men was Oxford or Cambridge. Indeed, these universities were almost perforce the main source during the whole of the last century because of the slow and late development of the other English universities.

As a result these men brought to the creation and running of the administrative system the norms and values that they had learnt during their own classical and humane education. Nor was the situation any different in Scotland, since the tradition of the Scottish universities was, if anything, more strongly in support of such an education. Therefore the educational system developed within the possible range of tolerance of the definition of the time under the influence of these men. The HMIs in particular did all they could to temper the business ideology of the time with humanity. As the system expanded in the twentieth century its administration continued to evolve in this tradition of general education and humane learning that these men had initiated and that the majority of their successors, many of them recruited from the same source, had learnt during their own education.

Local Education Authorities

It was not until the passing of the Elementary Education Act in 1870 (1872 for Scotland) that the state began to provide schools in Britain and even then this was not done directly, but through local agencies. Initially, locally elected bodies, the School Boards, were created especially for this purpose, since the goal was to give each area as much independence as possible to meet its own local needs. The number of such bodies was very large. In England and Wales there were over 2,500 School Boards and in Scotland, because of the dispersed nature of the population, over 950 Boards existed. As the system grew, the task of administration became more complex and successive Acts reduced the number of local administrative units. In 1902 the School Boards were abolished in England and replaced by 315 Local Education Authorities (LEAs). Similar arrangements were made in Scotland in 1918 when the School Boards were amalgamated into 37 bodies which, in 1929, became LEAs. In 1944 these numbers were reduced even further to 146 in England and Wales. The situation remained unchanged in Scotland.

Just as the establishment of the central organisation that has developed into the present DES led to the creation of positions to be filled and roles to be played, so at local level the delegation of much freedom to those bodies that became LEAs has encouraged the development of local educational bureaucracies. Firstly, there are the elected representatives of local electors. The Council delegates its educational powers to an Education Committee consisting of Councillors or Aldermen who can and do co-opt to their committee such interested persons as local educationalists or trade unionists. This primarily elected body of laymen, has, by law, to appoint a Director of Education to act as their professional adviser as the head of the office that administers and co-ordinates the local provision of education. These local government officers form a local civil service consisting of administrators and inspectors (Lester Smith, 20).

The source from which the members of both the Education Committee and their officers are recruited has an important influence on the way in which they fill their positions. The political complexion of the majority party on the local council is vital, but increasingly both Labour and Conservative councillors tend to be former grammar school pupils and hence to have common norms and values about many educational matters. By tradition those supervising local education in Britain have always served as teachers prior to their appointment as administrators and usually are graduates. They have a deep professional knowledge of the practical side of the schools and of teaching as well as usually being heirs to the humane classical tradition of British education. They tend, therefore, to run the educational system so as to perpetuate this spirit and to ensure as large a measure of freedom for the schools as is administratively possible. In this way, the local educational bureaucracy has developed in much the same manner as has the central administration.

The role of administrator at local level is a difficult one because of the many differing expectations of those in his ROLE-SET, that is those who play roles that interlock with the central role under consideration. Much work in the USA has shown that administrators, heads, teachers and school board members (equivalent in many ways to members of British Education Committees) do not have an agreed view of how administrators should behave in such specific situations as decisions on whether complaints by teachers should by-pass heads or on who should choose school text-books (Corwin, 8).

A key decision for the members of any organisation has to be made when a new leader is appointed. The Education Committee faces such a problem when it selects a new Director of Education. If American evidence is relevant it seems that whether or not the successor is recruited from inside or outside the organisation is crucial as an indication of the Committee's goal for the future of the organisation. To choose an 'insider' seems to mean that the present state of the system is considered satisfactory and a man is wanted who will maintain the present pattern and its goals. To appoint an 'outsider' can mean satisfaction, but is more likely to indicate that the Committee is searching for an innovator, someone who will not be tied by present conventions in his attempt to change the system.[1]

Governing bodies

There is a constant tension between administrators, whether central or local, and the schools themselves. The derogatory way in which teachers often speak of 'the office' is symbolic of this. Administrative decisions taken at what seems to be a great distance are the more difficult to suffer in the British system where a measure of trust and independence is given to each school (Clark, 7). It was partly in an attempt to preserve this independence that governing bodies became so important, particularly in England.

By the 1944 Act all secondary schools must have Boards of Governors and all primary schools Boards of Managers. When the principles of this Act were applied to Scotland in 1945, this provision was not extended to Scottish schools, though independent schools in that country do have such boards. As has been seen the Scottish educational system had developed in such a way as to make such organisation seem unnecessary. Very little is yet known of the way in which this legislation has been implemented. It would seem that, though the positions of governor and manager have been created by law, they are not always filled and that the methods of filling these positions vary greatly from place to place. However, recent work throws some light upon this problem (Plowden, 26).

Secondary schools would seem to have governing bodies more often than primary schools though some schools apparently have no such arrangements whatsoever despite the law. In the County Boroughs, where population is dense, schools are spatially close together and it is common to group several schools, often of varied type, under one governing body; on the other hand, in the areas run by County Councils where schools are scattered, each school tends to have its own Board of Governors or Managers. The members of these bodies are recruited from three main sources. There are, firstly, political nominees, usually elected members of the local government authority; secondly, as might be expected in a country where religious goals have been so important, there are clergymen, perhaps guarding the interests of the sect that originally founded the school or of a major local denomination; lastly, there are often representatives of parents. In general, governors drawn from these sources will tend to be rather conservative and defensive, though this may well be apt in view of the present functions of governing bodies. Their powers are not great, unlike the governors of independent schools who have great authority over the finances of their school. The LEAs exercise financial control, but governors do often share in the appointment of a new head, thereby exercising some control at a crucial point in the development of their school, since they may wish to choose a head who will change the goals of the school. These boards of governors or managers, in the main, function in a rather paradoxical way to link their schools to the local community and education authority while at the same time ensuring their independence *vis-à-vis* the LEA and parents.

EDUCATIONAL INSTITUTIONS

The Schools

The organisation of any school is very much determined by the goals given to it. These alter through time as the social definition of education, or that part of it relevant to the type of school under consideration, changes. In chapter 6 the way that goals influence the internal organisation of schools will be discussed. Here the aim is to look briefly at the way in which the present system of school types evolved. Up to the reorganisation of education in 1944–5 there were three parallel systems of schools in Britain. There was, firstly, a private sector, consisting of fee-paying preparatory and public schools. For very many of the former pupils of these schools their first experience of an educational institution even partly subsidised by the state was gained when they entered a university. The vast majority of the population, however, went through the state schools which were organised into two parallel systems.

There were the elementary and the secondary schools, run on separate codes, the former a cheaper version of education than the latter. There was a narrow but, under the growing impact of egalitarianism, increasingly strong link between the two. The basis of this mode of organisation has been referred to as 'sponsorship' (Turner, 38). The selective secondary (grammar) school was for the élite and entry to it assumed future membership of the élite. Thus those who passed the examination at eleven plus for entry to the grammar school, whether as fee-payers or as scholarship winners from the elementary school, were sponsored for their future social status. Those who went through the elementary system were not destined for high places; it was assumed that they were out of the 'contest'. A very few people did find it possible to go through the elementary schools and on to university, but this was not the usual route for moving up the social class system.

The goal of egalitarianism was of great importance in the reorganisation of 1944–5. A major clause in the Acts laid down that the two parallel systems should be abolished and be replaced by the successive stages of primary and secondary education.

The aim was to give secondary education to all in schools which had equality of esteem. The new secondary system was to be built out of three school types that had existed before and that had catered for the older age ranges of children. This tripartite system had developed historically and consisted of the grammar, technical and modern schools. The grammar school was for the élite; the technical school had certain economic goals, since its pupils looked to the middle ranges of the labour force; and the modern school was for the remaining children.

During the 1950s, the hopes that each type of secondary school would be given parity of esteem were seen to be illusory and in a spirit of greater egalitarianism a demand grew for a comprehensive or common secondary school to which all pupils in any catchment area should go. One of the main reasons that equal esteem was not won by the different types of school was that their goals altered under the influence of their clients or rather of the parents. This process will be discussed later in this chapter when we consider the ways in which the goals of educational organisations come to change.

The Colleges of Education

There are two main sources of teachers in Britain, namely the universities and the former training colleges, now called colleges of education. The colleges are the main source in England and Wales: in 1964 60·8% of the men and 76·5% of the women teachers in service had been trained in such institutions. In Scotland the proportion of graduate teachers is somewhat higher since they alone may teach in secondary schools of any type and many men and women with Ordinary degrees become primary teachers. In the mid-1960s only about a third of men and two-thirds of women teachers were non-graduates. This difference is largely attributable to the very long and close connection between the Scottish schools and the universities.

The goal of allowing maximum independence to schools can only be pursued if there is some assurance that teachers will not be excessively innovatory so that they redefine education outside the range of tolerance permitted by society at the time. Freedom is only allowed to the extent that they teach those subjects and use those methods that are generally approved. Therefore the machinery for training teachers is a vital part of the British school system since it has the responsibility for ensuring that the teachers hold the norms and values needed to maintain the system somewhere near to its present pattern. This process of initiating teachers into their future role is an example of what sociologists call 'professional SOCIALISATION' and will be examined in more detail in chapter 5.

The training colleges were originally established in the mid-nineteenth century. As the state provision of elementary schools grew so the demand for teachers rose. At the time all the colleges were run by religious denominations. They were deeply influenced by the low contemporary status of elementary education and by the religious goals of all education. As one result of the 1902 Act LEAs were allowed to establish colleges. These were built largely in the image of the older denominational colleges. They were small and, therefore, the pastoral care of students, especially women, was easier. They were often situated in rural areas; again, control of students was more complete, since it was difficult for students to go home or even to visit nearby towns. Thus, the transmission by the college of their image of the role of the teacher was facilitated as the chance of contamination from the world outside was small.

Since 1945 the status of the colleges has changed greatly. The egalitarian spirit of the times has worked to give equal qualifications to those who reach equal academic standards. Since work comparable to the standard of that needed for degrees was being done in the colleges, they have been given a status nearer to that of the universities. As a symbol of this they are now known as colleges of education and are able to teach some of their students to degree level. In addition, the priority given to education has risen, largely because of the new importance of economic goals, and this has aggravated the shortage of teachers already existing because of the rising population. As a result, the colleges are now larger, more often run by wealthy LEAs than the now rather poor denominations, and are more often in urban than rural areas, so that it would seem that their output, the teachers of the future, will be more like the general population than were the teachers of the past. The effect of this on the schools and their pupils is still a matter for conjecture.

The Universities

The universities form the main source from which is recruited those who run the British educational system as well as, especially in Scotland, the majority of secondary teachers. Almost all the administrative grade of the civil servants in the DES and the SED, the vast majority of HMIs and of the senior staff of LEAs are university graduates. This fact emphasises a very important difference between the educational system and many other sectors of British society. By its very nature education is something of a closed system. It feeds back its own products into itself. Since those who gain university degrees are very often those who excel by the criteria of the educational system, they tend to bring back to running the system the same values that they learnt when pupils of the system. Therefore a feed-back process of a conservative nature is inherent in the system and this helps to maintain the existing structural and normative pattern.

Yet much innovation springs from the universities because, over the last century, research and the creation of fresh ideas in all intellectual fields has come to be one of their main functions. Therefore the preservation of academic independence became a central problem of organisation when early in this century the universities began to accept substantial subsidies from the government. In 1919 the University Grants Committee (UGC) was established. The government gave monies to this body who distributed these to the universities, but did so without being accountable in detail to the Treasury. The members of the UGC were mainly eminent academics and thus could be trusted by both the government and the universities to distribute these subsidies with an eye to the often opposed goals of efficient usage and of academic interest. In the 1960s the sums given to the UGC have become so great that the goal of economy is coming to outweigh that of independence in the minds of many influential people, with the result that in 1967 arrangements for increasing the degree of accountability of the universities were made.

Increasingly in this century the goal given to the universities has changed from the traditional one of giving a humane education that would develop the individual to one which puts a greater stress on social needs, and more particularly on those of industry. Money has been channelled through the UGC to build new pure and applied science faculties, and to create technological universities even in Scotland where the appeal of a general education is still strong. This has altered the balance between faculties and hence the ethos of the universities. In addition, there has been a demand that the universities should be less élitist and open their doors more freely to all social classes. The considerable efforts made by the universities to achieve this have greatly increased the numbers of working class students, but the proportion of such students seems to be much the same as in 1945. However, the larger numbers of the working class at universities and the increased proportion of science students seems to have altered the atmosphere of higher education and this could well mean that the recruits to educational administration and to teaching have a different set of values compared with those recruited before the war. This could be an influence for change offsetting the conservative tendency referred to at the start of this section.

GOAL CHANGING

The topic of change has now been introduced. There are, as has been indicated, very strong influences towards organisational stability in education. The effect of recruitment from the system itself has been stressed. In addition educational institutions have a lower failure rate than do industrial organisations since they do not face bankruptcy in the same way. The constant balancing of profit and loss does not press on a school in the same way as it does on an industrial company. From the analysis so far, an important influence for change is clearly seen to be the constant dialogue of public and political debate at national and local level whereby goals are set for schools. At national level, formal or informal definitions of education evolve through debates in parliament or the press and under the impact of informed comment, perhaps from the representations of the teachers' professional associations. Particularly important are the Central Advisory

Councils whose redefinitions to meet the changing importance of social institutions have been so important in setting the goals of education during this century (Musgrave, 24).

These are all influences external to the educational system that result in organisational change within the schools so that a new bureaucratic structure must be established to meet the new goals. New positions, for example HMIs responsible for the teaching of economics or aides to primary teachers, are created. Or the role expectations for teachers change; teachers may have to stress their welfare work more than their academic tasks. One problem is that in all formal organisations once a change is made a new routine tends to be established so that further change is difficult. Therefore positive action is often needed at the national level to move educational institutions towards further essential change. Leadership for this can come through voluntary relationships between public organisations and private groups. Such 'inter-agency compacts' can successfully set new goals, especially if grants of money can be used as a lever.[2] In this way British industry moved the public schools towards a curriculum with a greater content of science by subscribing to the Industrial Fund during the 1950s. This fund was available to these schools on certain conditions of self-help. More recently much change in the curriculum and methods of the teaching of mathematics, science and modern languages has been initiated by research grants from the Nuffield Foundation. Research groups are rarely built into the educational structure in Britain, though some LEAs (for example, Surrey) have achieved a quicker adaptation to educational change by establishing a series of research committees with membership recruited from the LEA, experts, and practising teachers in various schools.

Though most of such change comes from outside the school some develops autonomously within the educational system – as LEAs, heads or teachers redefine education within contemporary tolerated limits or even create new definitions that are acceptable to society. In the 1930s the Director of Education for Cambridgeshire created a new type of school, the Village College; teachers have used new methods in, for example, teaching physics that have spread to other schools. However, one force for change that is a mixture of internal and external influences is at work in any school, namely the clients. The children, or their parents, can bring about a redefinition of the goals held by those running the school. This should occur more easily in independent schools where parents can withdraw their custom if they cannot buy the education that they want for their children, but very telling examples of this process can be cited from the state system. An obvious example is that further education for adults operates in a type of market economy.[3] If a large enough number of clients want an evening class in psychology or making pottery, then usually it will be supplied.

The same process has worked with surprising potency since 1945 to destroy one of the main assumptions upon which the implementation of the 1944 Act was built. The goal of egalitarianism meant that parity of esteem should be given to the three types of secondary school. Yet, since the clients of the modern school came mainly from a low social class of origin and were destined for jobs in the labour force that carried low status, parity of esteem was not given to these schools despite all the attempts of heads to earn equal status with other secondary schools (W. Taylor, 27). The goal given was undoubtedly impossible of achievement because of the social class of the clients. Again, the technical school was originally seen as one type of secondary education in its own right to suit a particular sort of child who was supposed to have practical abilities and interests. Middle-class parents soon realised that these schools, when entry was at thirteen plus, offered a second chance to recoup a failure to gain a grammar school place at eleven plus; working class parents saw that, whether entry was at eleven or thirteen, technical schools offered a sure way to a secure job, often of relatively high status. In this case the client intentionally changed the goals of the school. Sometimes machinery is specially created to achieve this purpose. The forming of a parent-teacher association or such a pressure group as an Association for the Advancement of State Education are examples. Organisations of this nature often seem to be dominated by the middle class and may, therefore, have goals appropriate to this class.

SUMMARY

Thus we see that the educational system is a complex structure created to meet definite goals, though often much of the existing structure is due to goals ruling in the past which may no longer be relevant. The nature of the system is such that the present pattern is securely maintained because recruits to the various positions have been socialised into the norms of the system. Change most often occurs under the influence of alterations in the values of the society in which the schools exist. Sometimes autonomous change develops within the system itself; this may take place within the tolerated limits of present definitions or, perhaps more rarely, creates a new, but acceptable, definition. This latter case is uncommon as only rarely do those working within the educational system consciously change the social values that govern the goals given to the schools.

NOTES

1. Carlson, R. O. 'Succession and Performance among School Superintendents', *Administrative Science Quarterly*, 6 (2) (September 1961).
2. Clark, B. R. 'Interorganisational Patterns in Education', *Administrative Science Quarterly*, 10 (2) (September 1965).
3. For an example in the U.S.A. see Clark, B. R., 'Organisational Adaptation and Precarious Values: A Case Study', *American Sociological Review*, **21** (3) (June 1956) (also in Etzioni, A. *Complex Organisations: A Sociological Reader* (Holt, Rinehart and Winston 1965).

FURTHER READING

Clark (7). Chapter 4, 'The Problem of Control', provides comparative American material and a conceptual framework for analysing the control of schools by local authorities.

Corwin (8). Chapter 8, 'Teachers as Professional Employees: Role Conflicts in the Public Schools', summarises much American work on various educational roles.

Lester Smith (20). Chapter 6, 'Some Thoughts about Administration', gives a brief account of the local administration of education.

Plowden Report (26). Appendix 13, 'The Management of Primary Schools', is one of the very few British accounts of the local administration of (English) education based on first-hand research.

Taylor (27). This book traces the way that the goals of the secondary modern school changed through the 1950s and the effect that this had within the schools themselves.

Turner (38). This paper is a near-classic analysis that compares the ideologies of social mobility in British and American schools.

4 The Role of the Head

In any organisation the most important figure is the leader since he is largely responsible for directing it towards the goals either that it is given or that he chooses for it. The role of the head must therefore be a focal point in any analysis of the formal organisation of a school. but the head becomes even more of a key figure in Britain than in most other countries since such stress is put on independence. The role of headteacher has been deeply influenced by the way that the role of the English headmaster developed in the nineteenth century. This chapter will, therefore, begin with a brief historical analysis of the role of the headmaster (Baron, 30). After considering the role under contemporary conditions a brief account will be given of the division of labour that has occurred as schools have grown in size; reference will be made to the roles of some of those who now assist the head in such specialised roles as deputy head.

A. THE HEAD

The History of the Role of Headmaster

Prior to about 1800 most schools were small; usually a school had only one master. In some cases masters were helped by assistants, usually called ushers, who had low status and were no more than aides; in boarding schools, for example they slept in the same room as the boys and were responsible for their behaviour out of the classroom. During the first half of the nineteenth century the public schools were reformed. Their numbers and their size grew to meet the demands of the new middle class whose wealth was created by England's industrial revolution. Thomas Arnold, headmaster of Rugby from 1828 to 1842, was an important influence on the way in which the reformed schools were organised. Like all headmasters of important schools at that time he was a clergyman and emphasised the pastoral care that he saw as implicit in the role of one who was in *loco parentis*. Much of his own personal power rested on CHARISMA, that is, on qualities peculiar to his own personality. Since the school had become large, he established boarding houses under house masters, who were often clergymen. To them he delegated much of the detailed work and care of the pupils. Furthermore, he gave substantial AUTHORITY to prefects chosen from among the older boys; this was done partly to render running the school more easy, but mainly to give them the chance to hold responsibility.

Arnold was much admired and his interpretation of the role of the headmaster was imitated widely. His was not the only answer to what was fundamentally a bureaucratic problem, namely how to run a school of a larger size than had previously been normal. Other solutions were tried. Thus, in some places the headship rotated among the masters, who each held it for a fixed period; in more democratic Scotland a committee system was sometimes found. Ultimately, Arnold's redefinition of the 'master' as 'headmaster' won the day and there followed in the public schools a series of great Victorian headmasters, mainly clergymen with strong and charismatic personalities.

During the second half of the nineteenth century the British school system was expanded to meet the new needs of the economy. Many fee-paying day schools were founded and a large proportion of the endowed grammar schools were reformed. Arnold's influence spread to those schools as headmasters imitated his methods. Partly, this was a simple process of diffusion of a new mode of organisation, but it was also important because it created a source of recruitment for the new generation of headmasters, many of whom had been both boys and masters at public schools. These men, on becoming heads, played their role as they had seen it played. Conditions favoured an easy acceptance of this idea of the role of the headmaster. Firstly, middle-class clients judged their children's schools by the laissez-faire ideology that ruled most of their views and therefore they equated this powerful independent leader with a business entrepreneur. This view seemed the more apt when the headmasters of the public schools formed the Headmasters' Conference (HMC) in 1869 to oppose government interference in private secondary education and, more especially, in the public schools. Another predisposing factor was that the endowments of many of the old grammar schools laid down that their 'masters' should be clergymen; therefore it was easy to envisage a minor Arnold as headmaster of such a school, even when reformed.

By the time that the LEAs were permitted to provide secondary schools as a result of the 1902 Act the Arnoldian tradition was firmly entrenched. The men who were recruited to the LEAs to administer the new secondary schools and those who were chosen both to fill the new positions of headmaster and to serve as masters under them were recruited from the public or proprietary secondary schools. They knew only one role model. Furthermore, men with this view came to staff the training colleges and to fill such positions as that of HMI. They were responsible for training the teachers for the elementary schools and a version of the Arnoldian role passed into the lower status stream of British education. In this way the influence has been passed down to all stages of the contemporary educational system.

The Contemporary Role of the Head

Any role may be considered from two viewpoints, from that of the actor and from that of those who interact with the actor in his role-set. As a result of the historical development of the role of the head there would seem to be a large measure of agreement on its definition. Each of the four goal areas has some relevance. Thus a head expects, and is given, a greater degree of independence in the planning of his school and its curriculum than in many other countries, though he is obviously constrained by such external influences as examinations and such social influences as the contemporary demands of the economy. He is seen, and sees himself, as having a pastoral responsibility for his pupils that would be unrecognised in most other European countries. Symbolic of this is the fact that the head takes morning assembly. This is the daily occasion for collective Christian worship and for whatever secular moral exhortation that the head considers necessary. A head is reckoned as good if he knows his pupils by name; he is supposed to know all equally well and favour none. He is expected to be a teacher rather than an administrator; the contrary is usually the case in large schools in the USA. Though his work load is unspecified a head, even where the administrative load is heavy, often teaches for three or four periods a week. Yet his is the responsibility for running the school and the task of using resources in as economical a way as is possible.

There is a stress on control of the children along several dimensions; for instance, the physical, moral, spiritual and social. But part of the responsibility for control is acknowledged to belong to others in the child's role-set. The extent of external responsibility varies with the type of school; boarding schools have a much greater degree of control in term-time than do day schools. However, any normal (i.e., excluding penal schools) type of school must today take much of the task of moral, physical and social control, though in some measure this may be delegated to such social agencies as the police or the Youth Service. Religious control is especially important to schools with religious foundations. Even in the schools provided by LEA's religion is more central than in, for example, American state schools.

Heads may control their pupils in the directions that they consider to be right by arousing their motivation. Success in examinations is often used as a way of making children work. Games may be organised by a school to teach its pupils loyalty to the school or some moral lesson, though the children may play willingly to meet some socially induced need of their own. In both these examples a common process for achieving control may be noted. An exchange process is at work. Both parties gain something wanted: the children gain the hope of a better job or status among their peers, while the school achieves an ordered existence.

In all these cases the head has freedom to interpret the goals given to him by those outside the school. These goals as given have been called his TASK. However, the head may perceive the task differently from those in his role-set. This perception has been termed his PROBLEM (Halpin, 13). A head's perception of what is expected of him is particularly liable to alter with the nature of the clients in his school.

Mothers of infants tend to be keener on their children's general welfare than on their academic success. As the children grow older and move up the primary school, parents with high aspirations for their children will want the head to organise his school so that there is relatively more stress on academic goals and less on general emotional or behavioural goals. Clearly, the social class composition of the catchment area will be important. A predominantly middle-class area will show more interest in what the school is trying to do than an area where the working class is more numerous (Herriott and St John, 18). Parents of children in the grammar school will begin to see education as important for future success in their children's career, while those with children in a modern school, particularly if they are in a low stream, will have ceased to bother, or will never have cared, about their children's schooling. At the moment little is known about how this process of influence from clients is working in comprehensive schools.

As has been indicated, most British schools are in many respects insulated from the views of those outside them, more especially because their profit and loss account is struck on a basis other than financial. In addition, the norm of independence has restricted the influence of parents even where parent-teacher associations exist. Yet it is extremely difficult for any head to ignore totally a redefinition of the goals of his school when this has been made and strongly pressed by the majority of his clients.

As a result of his definition of the 'problem' any head has two sets of decisions to make. The first relates to administrative details and follows from the particular way in which he emphasises and orders the priorities that are inherent in his perception of the task given to the school. This may be called the INSTRUMENTAL dimension of his role. It will include decisions relating to the curriculum, the time-table, external examinations and streaming. The second dimension may be termed EXPRESSIVE and refers to decisions relating to the maintenance of the emotional equilibrium of the staff and pupils. Examples of expressive decisions are the steps taken to smooth quarrels and friction among staff, the arrangement made to ease unpopular changes in rules amongst staff and children, the organisation established to allow parents to see staff, and the facilities provided in the school, whether curricular or extra-curricular, to gain allegiance of the pupils to the goals of the school as the head sees them.

Heads give differing emphases to these two dimensions. Thus a head who puts great stress on the instrumental dimension but gives small place to the expressive dimension may be called a martinet, while another head who gives the opposite emphases by stressing the expressive and ignoring the instrumental may be seen as permissive. Various combinations of emphasis are possible and each will result in a different interpretation of the role of head. Each particular style of leadership has an effect on how those outside the organisation see the school and on how closely they identify with it. This in turn could affect the support that, for instance, parents are likely to give to what the head is trying to do for their children. The head's leadership role will also affect the closeness with which his staff relate to the school.[1] It could well be that styles of leadership have measurable outcomes – in the case of the clients in the rate of drop-out and in the case of the teachers in the rate of turnover of staff.

Many heads derive much of their power from a charismatic personality in a manner reminiscent of their famous predecessors of the nineteenth century. However, as the size of schools increases, heads tend to rest their power more on their formal bureaucratic position. Yet all heads have great power resources that they can use in exchange for obedience and allegiance of staff and pupils. This is an important point to make since teaching is in many ways a profession; teachers, therefore, tend to claim, and to be given, much freedom of decision in the application of their skills to their very complex work. The head can use as one of his weapons the fact that the teacher will invariably have to ask him for a written reference if he wants to move to another job. The absence of such a document will lead to doubts about a teacher's competence by a potential employer. A head also has some control over the salaries of his staff, since he can recommend teachers for responsibility allowances. He has many resources for control that he can deploy as he makes instrumental decisions; he can, for instance, allocate quiet or noisy, well or badly equipped classrooms to teachers, give them more or fewer spare periods for correcting and preparing lessons, and allocate new or old books and equipment to them.

In the same way a head has resources that he can exchange for his pupils' obedience, He can refuse to allocate them to courses that seem vital to their further education. His written or oral references count for seeking positions in industry or in higher education or even in dealings with the police. In the case of pupils he also has the ultimate sanction of coercion by corporal punishment. Much of the way in which a head uses his resources for power and in general fills his role will be influenced by the source from which he has been recruited.

Recruitment to the Role

The influence of the public schools is strongly felt in Britain. These schools still recruit mainly from their traditional sources. In a recent sample of 84 headmasters of HMC schools, 62% had degrees in either classics (41) or history (21) and of these men all except one had a degree from Oxford or Cambridge (Weinberg, 29). So, despite the headmaster's pastoral role, grammar schools find support for appointing 'men of knowledge' in the academic tradition rather than 'child centred' teachers. Secondary modern schools do not recruit so many of their heads from among graduates, though the proportion appears to be rising; in Scotland, it must be noted, all heads of secondary schools are graduates including those of non-selective schools. The non-graduates tend to be more expressive in their leadership both because of their training and because of the influence of their clients. Many of the children in non-selective schools in which non-graduates teach do not want, or perhaps need, an academic education. Often their schooling has deteriorated into a custodial holding operation until they reach the minimum school-leaving age. Some graduates can adapt to this situation, but the appointment of a graduate as head in such a situation may be undesirable because the culture gap between some graduates and such children can be too big to bridge. In comprehensive schools size may tempt the head to become an administrator rather than a teacher, an atypical development in Britain; however, less is known about the role of the head in the comprehensive school than in the other school types.

In primary schools, most heads are non-graduates and were prepared in training colleges to be child-centred teachers. This source of recruitment, together with the fact that their schools are often still associated in people's minds with the former elementary schools, has given the heads of primary schools a somewhat lower status than heads of secondary schools. This is reflected in the fact that in many areas they are called 'headteachers' rather than 'headmasters'. This is also true for some modern school heads for the same reasons. Graduate heads are more common in Scottish primary schools than in England, though in the latter country the numbers seem to be rising.

It is not just the source of recruitment that affects how a head plays his role, but also the career pattern that he has followed to reach his present position. This will affect the knowledge and the attitudes that he brings to his new post. After his first appointment a typical pattern might be that a young teacher may change his job after a couple of years merely to gain experience and then be given a graded post; he might next move to gain the headship of a department. It is unusual for the heads of grammar schools to have been deputy heads; this is more common among modern school and primary heads, though it would appear to be more common in Scotland than in England. In addition, heads seem to be appointed at an earlier age in England than in Scotland. During his career a head will have gained a considerable body of experience of dealing with staff and children, and will have been well socialised into the professional norms. But, since it is extremely rare for teachers to be appointed as heads of the schools in which they have taught, there is some scope for a new head to bring a degree of change to the school to which he has been appointed, if only because he represents a younger generation than his predecessor.

Though little is known of the career patterns of those who become heads, one thing is clear: the position is gained by success in another role, that of teacher. Heads make their name by proving their expertise in teaching, whereas they have to exhibit very different qualities to succeed in the position of head. Their role is becoming much more that of an administrator as the size of schools grows even though the LEA itself carries much of his administrative burden; for example, much ordering of such educational materials as text books and stationery is carried out centrally rather than by individual schools. Certainly one dimension of his role has assumed great importance. He has to act as the co-ordinator of several heads of department, office workers and some domestic staff. Furthermore, he must learn his role on the job, since courses of instruction for new heads are as yet rare in Britain. Heads are socialised into their role. Since there is a range of tolerated behaviour, any new head meets conflict as he learns his role. His perception of his task will usually differ from that of his role-set and particularly from that of his staff who will rest their interpretation largely on the behaviour of his predecessor. Eventually a head may be so thoroughly imbued with the demands of his administrative role that his original goals are displaced. He may come to see his task with the orientation of business ideology rather than with that of the child-centred teacher or the man of knowledge. Bureaucratic replace educational answers.

An Analytical Framework

The diagram (Taylor, 37) opposite will act as a brief summary of much that has been said here about the role of the head. The two axes are drawn along the dimensions already described, namely instrumental/expressive and academic/administrative. From the examples already given it is easy to see the move from the academic/expressive head of the traditional small school where the head knew all the names of his pupils to the administrative/instrumental head of the contemporary big school to whom the turnover rate of the domestic staff may loom as a larger issue than the crime rate of the children.

ANCILLARY ROLES

Some indication of the growth in the size of schools is seen in the fact that the number of schools in England and Wales with over 800 pupils increased from 55 to 406 between 1954 and 1964. A

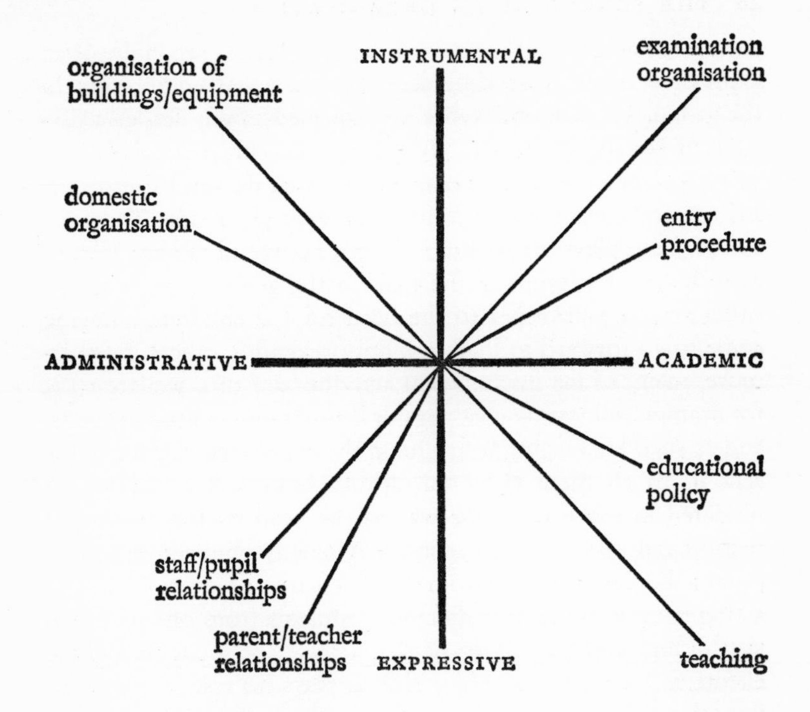

consequence has been that specific parts of the former role of the head have now DIFFERENTIATED off to form such separate roles as that of the deputy head, the careers master and the secretary to the head. In this respect it should be noted that an educational organisation is in one important respect very different from most formal organisations. The proportion of professionals who are expected to make decisions over a wide range of behaviour is very great. The chain of authority between the professionals and the leader is short. Only a small part of the personnel in the organisation is characterised by the long chain of command typical of, for instance, a factory. This final section is concerned with roles that lengthen the lines of authority.

The Deputy Head[2]

The role of the deputy head is rarely exactly specified, but his work is mainly in the expressive dimension. Groups seem to need two types of leadership: firstly, of an instrumental nature that focuses on achieving the goals of the group; and, secondly, of an expressive nature that maintains the emotional equilibrium of the group. Though both types are expected in any leader a division of labour of leadership function can occur, particularly as a group grows in size. In schools it seems that the head stresses the instrumental and the deputy head the expressive side. Thus, the deputy head plays the part of mediator between head and staff so as to keep the support of the staff for the goals of the head; he often acts as gatekeeper to the head for the children, allowing some to go forward to the head, but preventing others. Furthermore, many of his instrumental activities are of a welfare type, for example, allocating coat pegs or making dinner arrangements, and as such are helping to maintain the expressive balance of the school. In all these tasks the deputy head will be helped or hindered in much the same way as the head by the differential recruitment of staff to his schools. A mainly graduate staffroom poses a different problem from one that is non-graduate or mixed; a single-sex staff presents different problems from one that consists of men and women teachers. Likewise, the social class of the clients will affect the way in which he plays his role. Another influence on the way the deputy head perceives his problem is the source of his own recruitment.

In a grammar school this role is a terminal one since further promotion is not common. One of the main criteria for appointment is long service. When a vacancy occurs, usually through death or retirement, external recruitment is rare. Thus, deputy heads tend to be older graduates who have been in the service of their school for some time and who have thoroughly learnt the norms of their school. As a consequence, they will tend to have a conservative influence. The role of deputy head in a modern school is more often a stepping stone on the way to a headship; promotion to it is at a younger age and on the basis of instrumental success. Thus, these deputy heads may be more likely to try to show their worth by changing things.

In practice, this role is difficult to play because it is not closely specified. However, the bigger the school, the easier it becomes for a deputy head to make a definite sphere of action for himself. Deputy heads seem to be more satisfied with their role in larger schools. Yet most feel the conflict that is implicit in their position because they are middlemen between staff and head, or between cliques of staff, or between pupils and head. Paradoxically, their resources of power are rooted in the source of their conflict since as mediators or gatekeepers they are in a position to influence those on both sides of them. The head can have a happy staff; children may see the head. Often it is the deputy head who has the power to bring such things to pass.

Other Ancillary Roles

There has been a growth in other positions to support the head as his role has become more complex. Two changes will be noted here, namely the appointment of school chaplains and of careers masters. Both these developments are worth noting because they have differentiated out of the Christian and lay pastoral responsibility of the head, parts of his role upon which the nineteenth century headmaster put such emphasis. Thomas Arnold insisted upon being his own chaplain. The head may still have overall responsibility in this area, but the details of services or morning assembly have often been handed to a religious expert. Also, the head more often relinquishes to a member of his staff the task of advising on occupational choice and hence, especially in selective secondary schools, the decision about the curriculum that a child will follow.

The final group of positions to be discussed are the service occupations; for example, those who provide lunches or keep the school clean. One such position, the school caretaker or janitor, demonstrates very clearly a characteristic of certain types of position. The janitor has a relatively low status, but also has a great deal of power over both teaching staff and children. This power is based upon his strategic location in the organisation. He has control over the supply of certain important technical facilities to the staff; he often, for example, controls the heat of classrooms or the repair of electric plugs or other equipment. Teachers without heat in winter or without electricity at a vital point in a lesson are put in an awkward position. The janitor has ready access to influential people and can control the flow to, for instance, the head of such information as the fact that cigarette ends have been found in the toilets or that members of staff allow their classrooms to be left in an excessively untidy state. It is on such a basis that those playing relatively lowly roles in organisations can exert power over those who ostensibly have great authority even of a charismatic type.

SUMMARY

Various attempts were made in the nineteenth century to solve the problem of how to co-ordinate the organisation of a large school. Eventually, the role of leader that was evolved to meet the needs of the English public schools was imitated in all types of British schools. The head was seen as a powerful and independent figure with wide pastoral responsibility for his pupils. The way in which any individual played this role varied according to the way in which he saw his goals. This, in its turn, depended upon such considerations as the source of the recruitment of the head and the clientele of his school.

This view of the role is still very influential; though there are forces at work today that may bring about a redefinition of the role of the head. Under contemporary conditions the administrative demands on the head have become greater mainly due to the further increase in the size of schools. The head now seems to put more stress on the instrumental and administrative dimensions of his role at the expense of the traditionally important expressive and academic dimensions. The almost inevitable consequence has been the differentiation of the role of the head. Deputy heads have been appointed who seem to take over part of the head's former role of expressive leader. Other ancillary roles of a more administrative nature have also evolved, mainly to meet the needs of larger schools. Several of these low status roles possess a common sociological property, and this is seen very clearly in the case of the school janitor, namely that they can use their low status as a resource for power.

NOTES

1. See Etzioni, A. 'Authority Structure and Organisational Effectiveness', *Administrative Science Quarterly*, 6 (1) (June 1959).
2. Burnham, P. S. 'The Deputy Head' (unpublished M.Ed. thesis, University of Leicester 1964).

FURTHER READING

Baron (30). This paper traces the historical development of the role of the headmaster in Britain from the early nineteenth century.

Halpin (13) In chapter 2, 'A Paradigm for Research on Administrative Behaviour', a theoretical framework is evolved which is used in empirical research in schools in Part III, 'Research in Administration'.

Herriott & St John (18). This account of empirical research in the USA shows clearly how the nature of its clients influences the staff of a school in many ways.

Taylor (37). In this paper one educational role, the principal of a college of education, is analysed and a conceptual framework developed that is applicable to other educational roles.

Weinberg (29). A case study in the application of organisation theory to an educational institution, namely the public school, which takes a good account of the historical influences on this type of school.

5 The Role of the Teacher

HISTORICAL INFLUENCES ON THE ROLE

The status and the expected behaviour of the teacher varies according to the type of school in which he serves. These differences are to a great extent a legacy of the former elementary and secondary codes. As a result of the 1944 Act this system was replaced by successive stages of education so that primary teachers everywhere now apparently have identical status. However, the old differential seems to be perpetuated at the secondary stage where the schoolmaster in the selective secondary school carries higher status and is expected to be more academic than the teacher in the non-selective school who is considered to have more of a custodial than academic role.

Certain other residues from the historical development of the role have affected all teachers to much the same extent. They are seen as educators in the humane tradition with a pastoral responsibility for the children that they teach. In the nineteenth century the public school master paid great attention to the development of 'character'. This part of the teacher's role is now enshrined in the 1944 Act which requires education 'to contribute towards the spiritual, moral, mental and physical development of the community'. In this phrase came together some of the important influences of nineteenth century educational history. The religious influence is clear. So also is the part given to games in British schools. By 1900 games were very generally linked with moral education and had come to be seen as a measure of moral worth. As this view spread to the state schools responsibility for the organisation of school games grew to be an accepted part of the role of teacher.

Intellectual development was important and was also written

into the 1944 Act since education was to be fitted to the 'age, ability and aptitude' of the child. The part of the teacher's role that deals with academic teaching has always been stressed despite the emphasis on the more general, pastoral aspects. Since 1945, however, the weight given to purely academic work has increased for a number of reasons. The demands of the economy for trained manpower have become prominent as Britain moves towards 'the technological society'. In consequence, success in examinations is now crucial and entry to selective secondary school is seen as the avenue to a good job. Success in the selection examination at eleven plus that leads to selective secondary education has become vital. Simultaneously, attention has been drawn to the eleven plus by the pressures for a less élitist society. Therefore, for both economic and egalitarian reasons, more weight has come to be given to a teacher's skill in imparting knowledge and intellectual skills as opposed to the other parts of this role.

In no other country has the individual teacher been given such freedom to act as he will in the classroom. But, there are two restrictions on this independence. Firstly, care must be taken in dealing with political issues so as to avoid the accusation of teaching propaganda. Secondly, as a result of the historical pattern of educational growth, a teacher's religious instruction must conform to the locally agreed syllabus in England and to 'use and wont' in Scotland. The teacher has much greater independence than is usual in, for example, the USA in his choice of what is taught, how he teaches, and the text-books to be used (Baron and Tropp, 3). This freedom is guarded in England by the administrative arrangements of governing and managing bodies for schools to which reference has already been made. Another aspect of this independence is seen in the way that teachers do their utmost to avoid entering each other's classrooms while work is in progress. Thus the norm of independence supports an isolation that is encouraged by certain structural features of the position of teacher, which must now be examined.

STRUCTURAL INFLUENCES ON THE ROLE

The behaviour of any incumbent of a position is governed to a great extent by his role-set. A teacher must interact with many others who have resources of power with which to control his behaviour.[1] Mention was made in the last chapter of the ways in which a head can exert pressure on a teacher to conform to his wishes. In addition, other members of his role-set can influence a teacher. If his colleagues feel that he is behaving as is expected of him, they will extend the co-operation to him that can be essential in his work with his pupils. If it is felt that he is not playing his role within the limits of expected behaviour, they may bring such sanctions to bear as sending classes to him late or not permitting the withdrawal from their lessons of children that he needs for teams, concerts or plays. Parents also can affect a teacher's actions; they may ask awkward questions through the head or even in public at a meeting of the parent-teacher association where one exists. HMIs have the power to report well or adversely on the work of a teacher and this can be particularly important to a young teacher nearing the completion of his period of probation. External examiners can give a good or a poor reputation to a teacher by passing or failing his pupils.

A teacher has to balance the demands of this complex pattern of power relationships (Wilson, 40). One mode of resolving the problem is to abridge his role. This is commonly achieved in Britain by giving as little responsibility to the parent as possible for what goes on in the school. Parent-teacher associations are less common in England than in the USA and the high status of education in Scotland has enabled the Scottish teacher to go further in abridging his role in this direction than has been the case in England. Undoubtedly, the isolation that was mentioned above is very important in this respect since it means that the normal daily work of the teacher is largely hidden from the members of his role-set.

So far, this isolation has been seen as purely normative; it has, in addition, important structural roots in the schools. For the greater part of his working day a teacher is the only adult amongst thirty or forty children. Even when he is not in his classroom, he is still one of relatively few adults in a world of children where it is childish things or affairs concerning school that really matter. The world of adults tends to be somewhat apart and in it the teacher is seen as a stranger. Furthermore, he is even something of a stranger in the world of children since he is the educated one amongst the uneducated many. For the children he links the present to the future and is, therefore, marginal to their future lives. In a geographical sense he also seems to be a stranger. The increasing degree of urbanisation in Britain means that few teachers in cities today live in the catchment areas of their schools. Even in rural areas teachers may commute from the nearest urban area. In addition teachers are often transients from the point of view of their pupils. Young men teachers move on to gain a better job or more experience on which to base their careers; young women teachers marry and leave teaching to have a family. This mobility does, however, make teachers less social strangers and more akin to members of other professions. Indeed, professional associations are one force that acts to counter the isolation of teachers. With their help teachers face the world from a position of greater strength even if, to some extent, they remain apart.

Those with whom a teacher interacts as he goes about his work have varied interests at stake and this fact builds the possibility of conflict into his position. The whole of the staff of a school may come into conflict with those outside the school because the goals implicit in their role may be at odds with the goals, conscious or unconscious, of those in the population immediately around the school. Thus teachers may put more stress on honesty or hard work than people who work in the local factories. Conflict can also exist within a school staff, especially as schools grow in size, since there is a tendency for more departments to be created whose work has to be co-ordinated. In other words, the role of teacher becomes more differentiated. Positions are created with specific interests to be defended; the teacher of classics, the games teacher, and the music or art teacher all have claims on the curricular and extra-curricular time of their pupils which have to be settled to their mutual satisfaction.

Every teacher will meet self-conflict as he determines how to behave in specific situations with his pupils. He has to play many other roles besides that of teacher. His responsibility for a school team, which implies umpiring or refereeing on Saturdays, will clash with his role as a family man. His anticipated future role as head may demand that he moves to another post at a crucial point in the development of some child in one of his classes. As a member of a professional association, he may have to decide whether to go on strike, thereby withdrawing his services from his pupils. The very diffuseness of his role makes each of these decisions difficult, since he sees himself as responsible for the education of the whole child.

The control that teachers have over their pupils is also very much influenced by structural factors. Different types of school achieve different degrees of control. In this respect schools may be categorised along two dimensions.[2] Firstly, the closure of the organisation, or degree to which outside influences can be excluded, must be considered; thus 'communal' institutions, e.g. monasteries, may be compared with 'associational' institutions, e.g. working men's clubs. On the second dimension the goals of the institution may be more concerned with the moral values of its clients as is the monastery or with such instrumental activities as making a living. Applying these dimensions to schools the following diagram categorises schools by the degree of 'totality' of their organisation:

		CLOSURE	
		COMMUNAL	ASSOCIATIONAL
GOALS	MORAL	A boarding school	A day secondary school
	INSTRUMENTAL	A naval training ship	A part-time technical college

Thus the more TOTAL an institution the school is, the greater the control is that teachers can exert. Likewise within each school type different organisational arrangements influence the role of the teacher. In primary schools teachers tend to teach the same class most of the time unlike in secondary schools where the pupils move from one specialist teacher to another. Thus to some extent the school class as well as the school can be seen as more or less of a total environment for its pupils. The degree of totality will be greater in the primary, than in the secondary classroom. In all these cases the role that finally emerges as the norm accepted by all concerned will be much affected by the nature of the pupils in that class and in the whole school.

THE CLIENTS

The manner in which a person plays a particular role is affected by the other roles that he brings to the situation under examination. Of these latent roles one of the most important is the sex role, since it is so central to the feeling of personal identity. Most teachers are men or women first and teachers second. This will influence their playing of the role of teacher. This point is of importance when considering the sex of their clients, especially at the secondary level. The majority of primary schools are coeducational, but many secondary schools take only boys or girls and recruit teachers of the same sex. Where cross-sex appointments are made a man teacher brings his latent sex-role to a position where the behaviour predominantly expected will be based on a latent feminine role. Tensions may arise in both the staffroom and the classroom. In coeducational schools such difficulties are less likely to occur among colleagues, but can happen when teaching pupils. This is the more true because adolescents in secondary schools are themselves of an age when they are becoming conscious of their own sex-roles. Teachers at this stage may have more problems with children of the opposite sex than with those of their own sex.

The age of the child is another important factor. Almost all teachers of infants are women and are expected to play a very expressive and motherlike version of the role of teacher to their pupils who have left their families for the first time. Their latent feminine role makes this an easy role to play. By the junior stage men, though still a minority, are more common. In 1964, 74.5% of all primary school teachers in England and Wales were women. The role is still diffuse and weighted towards the expressive side, but men are often found with the classes of older children where control is becoming more of a problem. About half of the heads of these schools are men. In secondary schools in 1964 39.9% of the teachers were women. At this stage, the role is more instrumental with specialists teaching single periods. Each teacher may have responsibility for the expressive dimension of one class of children, whom they may never in fact teach; they merely meet their classes at registration and exercise a pastoral care as class teachers. One particularly British role is found mainly in selective secondary schools, namely that of sixth-form teacher. This teacher is a specialist having close links with the universities to which his pupils often go and from one of which he himself came. He has an intimate relationship with his pupils, who themselves have a social responsibility for younger pupils in their role as prefects.[3]

The wide interpretation put on the role of teacher in Britain means that unless teachers and taught have a large measure of agreement on values, conflict will make difficult the playing of this role in its fullest sense. Such clashes are most likely where teachers try to pass on basic values that are very different from those of their clients, whether this refers to the pupils or their parents. Teachers tend to have middle class values because of their class of origin or because, though born as working class, they aspire to be middle class. Therefore conflict is more likely where the pupils are largely working class. This is especially the case in urban areas and in non-selective secondary schools. Teaching in a secondary modern school in the centre of a large city can be a frustrating and unsatisfactory experience for many teachers. Two consequences can follow. Firstly, a teacher may abridge his role so as to concentrate on the instrumental dimension together with, especially in the case of boys, such activities as games where a measure of common ground exists. Secondly, and more directly measurable, he may seek a more congenial post elsewhere. In primary schools turnover of staff in the early 1960's was directly related to size of school, and since the largest schools are in urban areas, this implies the highest rate of turnover in the cities. A similar situation existed in secondary schools where one survey showed that by 1961 modern schools in slum areas had only retained 39% of the staffs that they had in 1959. It should be added that the role of teacher in such schools is made no easier by the rate of turnover of pupils; in one primary school 111 out of 150 children were 'recent newcomers'.[4]

Since there is a correlation between social class and measured ability, schools catering mainly for a clientele of low social class will tend to have a lower level of measured ability. Therefore unselective secondary schools will be less attractive to teachers who see themselves as men of knowledge. This factor relating to ability can reinforce that dependent upon values, that has just been described. Much will depend upon the source of recruitment of teachers to such schools since this will to a large extent determine the image that they have of themselves.

RECRUITMENT

Mention has already been made of the sex pattern of recruitment. The younger the children, the more likely their teachers are to be women. Historically, social class has been an important factor since, until about 1944, the ambition of many an able working-class youth was to become an elementary school teacher and so move into the middle class. In Scotland the whole of the teaching profession was, and probably still is, a recognised avenue for moving up in social status. In consequence, teachers tended to hold strongly to middle-class values. Since 1944, there has been a tendency for the profession to recruit rather more from the middle class than previously (Floud & Scott, 12). Therefore, the experiences and values which young people bring to the role of teacher may still be rooted in the middle class. This could make it even more difficult to bridge the gap between the norms of teachers and their pupils in schools where pupils are predominantly working class.

Teachers are recruited from two main sources in Britain, namely from the universities and the colleges of education. The majority of English university graduates who enter teaching receive a year's professional training between taking their degree and starting to teach; in Scotland, no graduate may teach without such training. However, there is a crucial difference between a graduate's training and that which the certificated teacher undergoes at a college of education. The former is trained subsequent to graduation; the latter is trained concurrently while he receives his advanced academic education. The orientation of the graduate tends, therefore, to be towards his academic discipline; hence, he has here been called 'a man of knowledge'. The certificated teacher has, however, usually been forced to think in terms of applying his knowledge to teaching children and has been taught by lecturers, invariably former teachers themselves, whose aim is, on the whole, to inculcate such a view; hence, the certificated teacher has here been called 'child-centred'.

Each type of school has a different pattern of recruitment. In 1964 the proportions of graduates by school type in England and Wales was as follows:

	men	*women*	*total*
Primary	7·8	3·0	4·2
Comprehensive	47·4	33·0	42·2
Secondary Modern	19·4	12·8	16·6
Secondary Technical	54·7	45·8	52·1
Secondary Grammar	80·4	71·4	76·8

It is clear that, at the secondary stage, the higher the status of the school, the greater the proportion of graduates on its staff. The predominance of 'men of knowledge' in selective schools and of child-centred teachers, especially women, in primary schools is clear.

When the structure of the educational system results in such differences, the hopes of achieving a unified teaching profession with common aims, so often expressed by the teachers' organisations, seem far-fetched (Musgrave, 22). These divisions are accentuated by the number of graded posts carrying salary increments that have been created in grammar schools to attract graduates, particularly mathematicians and scientists, to teach children due to take the external examinations now seen as vital on economic grounds. These posts have, however, established a more formal career line in the schools than was the case before the war. The exact pattern of the career of the typical British teacher in the various types of school is as yet unexplored. One deduction can be made from the figures of turnover in slum schools. As was found in Chicago under similar circumstances,[5] it seems that many teachers move horizontally out of schools in poor areas into posts of the same status prior to moving vertically to a post of higher status.

The two types of teacher so far described will have different motivation in filling their role. The child-centred teacher will put more weight on the expressive dimension and the man of knowledge will stress things academic. Thus, a recent survey found that when undergraduates in their final year ranked the type of school in which they would like to teach the following order emerged: grammar sixth form, grammar generally, comprehensive, modern, junior and infant.[6] Within both categories of teacher there are what may be termed second choice teachers whose original goal was to enter some other career. Their motivation may be warped by this factor. Such teachers, when graduates, may put even more stress on the academic side and less on their pupils as persons; those who are certificated may do the same since many appear to be those who were disappointed in reaching universities and hence are failed men of knowledge.

There is, in addition, a third type of teacher, the missionary, whose aim is almost entirely to save his pupils from their social circumstances. When a head has the power to choose his staff, he will try to appoint whichever of the three types matches the clients of his school. For his sixth form, the head of a public school will want the scholar who would be out of place in a slum modern school where a missionary might be more apt, though a tough child-centred teacher could serve with equal success.

THE ROLE IN PRACTICE TODAY

A number of recent studies allow an assessment to be made of the role of the teacher in contemporary Britain (Westwood, 39). So far, an implicit assumption has been that there is agreement about the expected behaviour of those who fill the position of teachers, both among teachers themselves and among those in their role-set. In fact the role of teacher may be divided into several sectors. One analysis (Finlayson & Cohen, 32) uses four sectors. The first concerns organisation: for example, whether or not the class is streamed and the amount of clerical work required of the teacher. The second sector covers the general aims held by the teacher with regard to such an important issue as the comparative emphasis to be given to the 3 Rs and to such pastoral functions as character building or social training. A third sector relates to the way in which the motivation of the pupils is gained. The classroom behaviour of the teacher forms the fourth sector; the way in which pupil and teacher interact with each other is an example of this category. This method of analysis only deals with the role of the teacher while actually teaching in the classroom. In the remainder of this section, consideration will be given to each of these four sectors, though two other important sectors exist. Firstly, there is that concerned with the behaviour of the teacher in school when not teaching (for example, when in the staffroom or on the games-field) and, secondly, that concerning the behaviour expected of the teacher when away from the school (for instance how the teacher should dress and spend leisure time).

Since the teacher's role includes so many complex sectors, it is not surprising that consensus in any one sector is apparently rare. If one considers the organisational sector, the evidence on streaming shows that there is considerable disagreement amongst teachers on how they should organise their classes for teaching purposes. In a sample of primary teachers in streamed schools, 45% were in favour of streaming, 45% were neutral and 10% were against this form of organisation, while in unstreamed schools 13% of the sample were in favour, 35% neutral and 52% against streaming.[7] Clearly, not only is there overall disagreement in this respect, but also there is considerable disagreement amongst teachers even in the same type of school.

The role-set of the teacher is so extensive that some disagreement might be expected, but there is evidence to show a lack of consensus at the core of the role-set, namely in the expectations held by teachers and parents about general educational aims (Musgrove and Taylor, 35). Teachers in both primary and secondary schools seem to stress intellectual and moral education while believing that parents wish to give priority to intellectual education and social advancement as the main aims of the school, at the expense of moral and social education. In fact, the parents questioned stressed the same aims as the teachers, namely intellectual and moral education, though working-class parents gave more emphasis to social advancement than did middle-class parents. The relationship between teachers and parents can only be made more difficult if they base their expectations of each other on disagreement due to ignorance.

Evidence on the influence of age on the way the British teacher plays his role is sparse and contradictory. Certainly, in the popular view there seems to be a cycle of stereotypes. The young teacher is seen as an anxious and idealistic recruit who, in time, becomes a relaxed and secure full member of his profession and ultimately grows into an old teacher, deferred to by new recruits about whose quality and views he in his turn complains. To investigate this progression is complicated by the fact that any teacher is simultaneously playing a number of roles and as he or she grows older will pass from playing the role of the young man or woman to that of a middle-aged and, ultimately, of an old person. The expected behaviour of the teacher may not change as much throughout his career as may the more general behaviour expected of the age grades through which the teacher passes.

These issues raise the problem of professional socialisation. In the sector of classroom behaviour, young teachers appear to be more 'permissive' than older teachers.[8] Yet it also seems that student teachers move (after their first year of training) to a peak of permissiveness in their second year, but by the completion of their training at the end of three years have returned to a position where they hold expectations about their classroom behaviour nearer to those of the head teachers under whom they will soon serve. There are, perhaps, two phases to this process of early professional socialisation. There is a preparatory phase during which skills and ideals are learnt. This is succeeded by a phase deeply affected by the meeting with organisational reality when theory is forgotten under trying practical experience (Finlayson and Cohen, 32). The progressive goals of the lecturer in the college of education are displaced by those of the practising teacher.

The power resources of the teacher are relevant to a consideration of the role sector that deals with motivating the child. The degree of physical or moral coercion that a teacher can use is governed by the norms of the society. In Scotland, in general, more corporal punishment is permitted than in most parts of England, though the relevant norms can and have changed through time. Teachers can also use coercion of a more utilitarian kind. They may use the fear of failure in an examination, the passing of which is vital for their pupils' future careers, in order to make children work in the classroom. There are a large number of power resources built into the way in which a teacher organises his class. He can use the arrangements for seating or grouping children to gain his pupils' favour by putting friends near one another. He can allocate greater or smaller amounts of attention to individual children thus gaining their favour. His marking system may be used to encourage the weaker brethren. In classes grouped by ability promotions or demotions, or more usually their threat, can be used to motivate children. Some teachers are able to use particular charismatic qualities of their own to stimulate pupils towards a desired educational goal; a good games player may teach Latin to some pupils more effectively than a first-rate scholar.

Whatever behaviour is expected in the contemporary British teacher, there is a difference from that expected in the nineteenth century when such extra duties as playing the church organ on Sunday were not unknown. The growing power of their professional associations has enabled teachers to abbreviate their role in this respect and the associations are still at work trying to delimit the role of the teacher. For example, in the organisational sector there are the questions of supervising dinners, of collecting National Savings and of whether aides should be employed to assist teachers with such auxiliary duties as helping children to change for games or distributing and collecting equipment for lessons. The role of the teacher is never static, but changes through time.

The final outcome of the teacher's role is what he achieves with his pupils. Attempts to measure his success tend to emphasise what can be counted, that is examination successes or the number of pupils staying at school beyond the minimum legal leaving age. Such a measurement ignores whole role sectors rated high in Britain, more especially the pastoral part of the teacher's role.

Furthermore, this stress on countable outcomes can lead to goal displacement. The means to education, for example examinations, may become ends in themselves. Merely to consider the problems implicit in any measurement of the outcome of the teacher's role makes even more clear the main burden of this chapter. There are many roles of the British teacher. Which is to be measured? There are primary teachers and secondary teachers. There are physical education and music teachers. The behaviour expected in each type of teacher, however, has in common whatever consensus exists in the school or in the educational system as a whole on the goals to be pursued in the process of teaching.

SUMMARY

The historical development of the role of teacher has resulted in teachers in secondary schools having somewhat higher status than their colleagues in primary schools. This fact is enshrined in the titles of 'teacher' and 'master' or 'mistress' which are still commonly distinguished today. Yet there is general agreement that in both cases a teacher should have a pastoral role and be free in his own classroom to teach as he will within the general framework of the humane tradition. Constraint is put upon the teacher by the complex nature of his role-set. To counteract outside influences teachers have tried to abridge their role and have created a norm whereby much of their daily work is hidden from public view. This isolation is increased by structural factors. The teacher's control of his pupils is similarly influenced. Thus the totality of the school is important. This varies by type of school; the contrast between a day and a boarding school is a clear example.

The nature of the clients of a school also influences the way that teachers play their role and the success they have in translating their goals into educational outcomes, inasmuch as these are measurable. Especially where the values of teacher and pupil are in conflict, as in many urban areas of contemporary Britain, teachers may be forced into changing their view of their role. The source of recruitment largely determines whether a teacher sees himself as a man of knowledge or as child-centred, since each of these types of teacher is socialised into his professional role in a different manner. Any full analysis must deal with the various sectors of this role, for instance, with the way the classroom is organised, the methods of teaching used and with the mode of the teacher's behaviour outside the school. It is clear that to speak of the role of the teacher in any unitary way is over simple.

NOTES

1. Becker, H. S. 'The Teacher in the Authority System of the Public School', *Journal of Educational Psychology*, **27** (April 1952) (reprinted in Etzioni, A. *Comparative Organisations: A Sociological Reader* (Holt, Rinehart and Winston 1963)).

2. Bidwell, C. E. & Vreeland, R. S. 'College Education and Moral Orientations: An Organisational Approach', *Administrative Science Quarterly*, 8 (2) (1964).

3. *15 to 18* (Crowther Report) Vol. I (H.M.S.O. 1959, pp. 222–5).

4. *Children and Their Primary Schools*, Plowden Report (H.M.S.O. 1967, Vol. I, p. 51 and Vol. II, p. 554); *Half Our Future*, Newsom Report (H.M.S.O. 1963, p. 246).

5. Becker, H. S. 'The Career of the Chicago Public School Teacher', *American Journal of Sociology*, **57** (5) (March 1952).

6. 'Undergraduates' Attitudes to Teaching', *Trends in Education*, **2** (April 1966, p. 17).

7. *Children and Their Primary Schools*, Plowden Report, Vol. II (H.M.S.O. 1967, p. 571).

8. *Children and Their Primary Schools*, Plowden Report, Vol. II (H.M.S.O. 1967, p. 561).

FURTHER READING

Baron & Tropp (3). This paper is one of the few comparative studies of the role of the teacher in the USA and England.

Finlayson & Cohen (32). The report of empirical research into the role of the teacher as seen by heads and by student teachers throughout their years in college.

Floud & Scott (12). The report of a survey into the social origins of teachers in schools in England and Wales in the mid-'50s.

Musgrave (22). Chapter 13, 'The Teacher in a Profession', considers the sociological nature of the professions and discusses the question of whether or not teaching is a profession.

Musgrove & Taylor (35). The report of empirical research among parents and practising teachers on the role of the teacher.

Westwood (39). A critical survey of the literature on the role of the teacher with a full bibliography.

Wilson (40). A theoretical sociological analysis of the role of the teacher.

6 The School

In the last two chapters we have examined the roles of the staff in various types of British school. In this and the next chapter the intention is to see how teachers organise schools and classrooms as they seek to achieve the goals given to the educational system of their country. In this chapter the stress is on the formal and informal organisation of the school, while in the next chapter the focus will be on the pupils themselves.

Schools can be viewed as organisations that are in some ways akin to factories. A parent implicitly makes a normative contract with a school; he agrees to exchange the submission of his child to the authority of the staff for certain services from them, for example a reasonable chance that the child will pass examinations or that he is looked after and fed well once between 9 am and 4 pm. Again, from the school's point of view, pupils are its input and former pupils its output or product. The character of the raw materials used by a factory affect the way in which it is organised, and much has been said so far to show how the input of a school, its clients, influence the way in which it runs. The output of a factory must meet the needs of the market at which it aims or bankruptcy will eventually ensue. Schools in the state system rarely close for analogous reasons, but, if their products do not meet the expectations that are held for that type of school, change must occur. Either the school must alter or the image of it held at large must change.

IMAGES OF SCHOOLS

The public have expectations of school types in much the same way that they hold expectations of positions within them. These images of schools are akin to role expectations. The staff may see the task given to a school in a different way from the public at large so that they have a different image of the school from that held by those outside it. This divergence in some ways parallels the differences about his expected behaviour that can occur between an individual and those in his role-set. Indeed, an organisation like a school has an ORGANISATION-SET, a concept akin to that of role-set. Those in each organisation that has dealings with a school may have a different image of that school type. Thus, members of the LEA, the parent-teacher association, the chamber of commerce and the trades council may all hold a different image of, for instance, a secondary modern school.

Very little is definitely known of the image of British schools. Margaret Mead (21) has described three generally accepted images of schools in the USA: the little red school-house, the academy and the city school. The British parallels could be the one-teacher country school, the grammar school and the modern school. The first image represents a school type rapidly disappearing in England, though still necessarily more common in Scotland where there are many areas of low population density. The other two schools are well enough established to have widely accepted and potent, though sociologically unexplored, images.

The contemporary grammar school has inherited the humane, élitist tradition of its past. Entry to this school sponsors a child for future membership of the élite. Recently the influence of egalitarianism has somewhat changed the image of the grammar school. The character of its clients has changed as the proportion of working class pupils has risen during this century. The previously accepted image is now no longer necessarily held by all entrants, and teachers have had problems in coping with first generation grammar school pupils whose image of their school differed from that of the staff and the majority of other clients. The other major influence for change has been that of the economy; the predominantly humane curriculum has given way to a greater emphasis on science as the economy becomes more firmly based on science and technology.

The modern school was created to implement the goals of the 1944 Act and was seen by educationalists, the informed public and many teachers as a full secondary school of a new type that had parity with the grammar school. The influence of its mainly working-class clients and the low status of the occupations which it served soon undermined this image of the modern school. This process was the easier as, to a large extent, the modern school inherited the already low status of the elementary school from which it seemed indistinguishable, since it often inherited the same buildings (W. Taylor, 27). As the drive for equality emphasised the importance of selection for grammar school, the staff of modern schools came to see their purpose as that of helping their pupils to adjust to failure or to overcome social disadvantages. Yet very often there was no agreement between clients or parents and teachers – or others with power – about the exact image of the secondary modern school.

The images of the other school types that have been created since 1945 are even less certain. Comprehensive schools tend to look new and be well equipped compared with many grammar schools; this could affect their public image. Primary schools have cast off much of the image of the elementary school from which they were born, and particularly in England, have inherited a tradition of progressive and child-centred education. Especially when in modern buildings, they have evolved an image of freedom and openness (Blyth, 6). In the latter case there may well be more agreement within their organisation-set about the image of the school merely because of the greater consensus on the need to stress expressive goals in the education of younger children.

THE SCHOOL AS A BUREAUCRACY

These images are powerful influences on the way that schools are organised. They help to determine the positions in them and the role expectations of those filling these positions. In this respect schools may be viewed as bureaucracies with a hierarchy of positions for which there are recognised training and educational standards; for instance, in England teachers with either a degree or a certificate may teach in secondary schools whereas in Scotland only those with a degree may do so. Promotion up the hierarchy is based on accepted criteria; prior to their appointment, headmasters must have taught for some years, the period varying somewhat by LEA. Much of the behaviour in educational positions is standardised according to formal or conventional rules; it is not, for instance, normal to criticise a colleague in the presence of pupils. As schools grow in size these criteria of bureaucracy are more clearly visible. Teachers divide the work and specialise so that heads of departments must be appointed. The lines of power are laid down through these departmental heads so that ultimate authority is centralised, though a head may, if he so wishes, delegate details in specific cases; a teacher can, for example, decide on the scale of rewards and punishments in his own class. The structure of the organisation may differ in shape according to the type of school and, if the school is growing in size, must be flexible enough to accommodate changes. Thus, in the recently developed very large comprehensive schools, house systems have been evolved under housemasters who draw special allowances for the responsibility involved.

In the case of a boarding school the same processes are at work, but there are additional problems. Since the institution is more nearly a total one, these problems of administration will be more complex. During term time the school cannot rely to the same extent as a day school can on the direct help of parents or of such local welfare agencies as family doctors or youth clubs. Therefore, a boarding school must contain additional positions to deal with these functions and the head may give greater stress to the pastoral sector of his role at the expense of the teaching sector.

There is evidence from high schools in the USA to suggest that size of school has certain automatic, but rather unexpected, results. The pupils in smaller high schools seem to take a larger number of academic subjects, to participate in more extracurricular activities and to hold more positions of responsibility in such activities. In very large (more than 2,000 pupils) high schools, though the academic and other facilities offered by the school are much richer, the participation of individual pupils seems to be narrower (Barker and Gump, 4). In general, in a smaller school the head can allocate staff and pupils to positions on the basis of personal knowledge, whereas in a large school where the teaching staff alone may number over a hundred, he must rely on the advice of his departmental heads for information about the skills and capacities of those under them. Likewise the head will have to consult his housemasters on the appointment to positions of responsibility of pupils whom he can often know only by name.

Access to the positions in any bureaucracy is governed by rules and by achievement. In the case of teachers this may mean service for a number of years that is recognised as efficient. Such a criterion as favouritism is rarely, at least openly, used. Throughout his career a teacher's performance is liable to constant assessment by the head and by colleagues. Relevant criteria may be the success of his pupils in external examinations or how much noise emanates from his classroom. A head is more likely to use the former criterion in choosing the head of a department and the latter in selecting a housemaster or a new form-master for a difficult class.

The pupils of a school may also allocate staff to such formal positions as chairman of a permanent school club or to such informal positions as organiser of an *ad hoc* dance, using their assessment of whatever qualities they feel apt for these positions. However, pupils are themselves under constant assessment with regard to their fitness for positions available in the future both within and outside the school. External examinations are important criteria both for careers after school and for the allocation of senior positions within the school, since to a great degree moral worth is judged in British schools by academic success. In addition participation and success in extracurricular activities, particularly in games, are used by British teachers as measures of the moral fitness of their pupils to fill such positions of responsibility in schools as that of prefect.

In general, such total institutions as prisons that aim to resocialise their members tend to get rid of their successes whereas those institutions like schools that socialise their members tend to get rid of their failures.[1] It is those pupils who do badly by the criteria of the schools who leave secondary modern schools at fifteen and grammar schools at sixteen. Since middle-class children tend to meet these criteria more easily and stay on at school longer than working-class children, it is not surprising to find that in two recent surveys 90% of the prefects in a secondary technical school and just under 80% of those in a comprehensive school were from middle-class homes.[2] Those who succeed become prefects as a reward for the way in which they have learnt the norms of their school. In this position, they act as assistants to the staff, though the educational aim is to prepare these pupils to hold positions of responsibility after leaving school. Certainly this position is one of difficulty as prefects are in great role conflict. They have constantly to decide whether to take the side of the other pupils among whom, in many ways, they are still numbered or of the staff from whom they draw their authority. In this respect their position resembles that of the classic marginal man, the foreman in industry.

THE ORGANISATIONAL FRAMEWORK

The particular structure that the bureaucracy takes in any school will be governed by the nature of its goals. Are they moral or technical? Can it be best described as a communal or an associational institution? Various organisational devices can be used to ensure that the roles of staff and pupils meet the goals implicit in the public image of any particular type of school. Most obvious are those of a spatial or temporal nature. Boarding schools are often marked by isolation as are penal institutions for adolescents; socialisation into new roles or resocialisation into roles that are socially approved are easier in a geographical situation where the pupil's role-set is severely abridged. The architectural character of school buildings can reinforce the goals implicit in certain forms of education; the progressive primary school, especially when sited in a modern building, usually has large windows, plenty of open space, colourful classrooms and furniture that is easily movable. The aim of freedom and creativity can more easily be achieved here than in the dull, constricting and inflexible classrooms of a traditional building. The length of the teaching period and the exact subject to be taught at any specified time may also be fixed, and this may characterise a rigid approach. Another temporal consideration is the length of the school day or term; the longer this is, the greater the period of control by the school over its pupils. Hence, boarding schools have long terms and penal schools have no holidays. In grammar schools, the effective length of the school day is lengthened by stressing such activities as games and meetings of societies that occur after official school hours have ended.

These latter devices whereby control is extended, may be analysed in a second way. Basically they are a means of increasing the number of officially approved roles available to pupils. The nature of such additional roles will be determined by the goals implicit in the type of school under consideration. In a selective secondary school aiming at preparing its pupils for the élite, the roles will be those like that of prefect that stress the development of the personality so that, it is hoped, responsibility will be more easily taken after leaving school. In a technical school, workshops and societies stressing practical science will be made available. In a primary school, general social responsibility will be stressed by the weekly rotation of such positions as monitor in charge of flowers or pets. Similarly, in the case of the curriculum, a greater or smaller emphasis may be put on the classics, science or religious instruction with the intention of producing young men and women who are more or less humanist, technical or religious (Dahlke, 10).

The role expected of pupils may be influenced by whether or not the positions made available to them by the mode of organisation of the school and its classes stress homogeneity or heterogeneity. If the emphasis is put on the likeness and the equality of human beings, then children of categories usually considered dissimilar will be placed together. It is usual to organise comprehensive schools, where equality is considered a main goal, on a coeducational basis, thereby to some extent minimising differences between the sexes. When children are put in classes that are not streamed by ability, the hope is that far less emphasis will be given to differences in the present state of their intellectual capacity. Again, in cities where the proportion of coloured children is high attempts are usually made to ensure an adequate mixture of white and coloured children in the schools with the aim of minimising such ethnic differences.

There are many acts in collective settings, other than those in such highly organised settings as classrooms, that are important in that they relate individuals to the social order both inside and outside the school. Particularly crucial in this respect is the ritual behaviour common in most British schools. Sociologists use the word RITUAL to refer to those more or less inflexible patterns of activity that have come to carry meaning beyond the context in which the specific act occurs. Ritual has an specially important place in transmitting the values implicit in the expressive order of any school; rituals that act in this way may be termed consensual, since they tend to bind the members of the school together. It is normal for a pupil to call a man teacher, 'sir'. This symbolises the hierarchy of power in the school and every time a teacher is so addressed, provided that a mocking tone is not used, the relationship of superiority/inferiority between the teacher and pupil is reinforced. Furthermore, there are overtones in this particular behaviour that relate the pupil to the value system external to the school so that he is also symbolically assenting to the superior position of the older person and, often, of someone who has higher social status, both norms which are commonly found outside the school.

Morning assembly usually serves a ritual function as well as being an act of worship. Even when the school has a chaplain, the head will normally take assembly, thereby symbolising the pastoral sector of his role. Very often the prefects will enter the hall after the rest of the school and sit apart, near to the head, thereby stressing their higher status and the source of their authority. The head will announce school sports results or the academic successes of pupils, thus indicating the collective pride that he wishes to create. He will also use the forces engendered in such a gathering to support his attempts to inculcate sentiments that the society supporting the school might wish to see transmitted. Worship together by pupils of several denominations and from all social classes may be seen as the symbol of a greater religious and social tolerance.

If rituals in the expressive order are cohesive, those in the instrumental order work for differentiation (Bernstein, Elvin and Peters, 31). Many groups exist in schools that are marked off from one another; there are, for instance, age and sex groups, and status groups such as prefects. In all these cases rituals grow up that reinforce this separateness. Older children are permitted, even within the limits of school uniform, to dress more informally and this marks their membership of a more influential age grade. Boys and girls, particularly at the primary stage, may enter school by separate entrances and have different playgrounds; this may well keep the 'rough' boys apart from the 'nice' girls, but it symbolises the process of sex typing that is beginning to assume importance in the latter stages of the primary school. This is especially true in Scotland, where children move to secondary school a year later than in England. Prefects in secondary schools usually have a room of their own; this comes to be viewed as the seat of much authority in the school.

In this last case another process that is at work can also be seen. Since the visibility of the prefects is increased by the ritual aspect of their separate room, the school finds it easier to encourage the growth of those attitudes towards authority that it hopes to inculcate. The house system is used in a similar way in day schools. These groupings of pupils are largely artificial, unlike the residential houses in boarding schools, but they are given names with emotional significance to create groups that will compete with one another the more fiercely and hence learn 'to play the game' or 'be loyal'. The examples so far given have been of prescriptive rituals, that is rituals that indicate what ought to happen. Proscriptive rituals or taboos are also possible; these indicate to children those things that it is hoped will not occur. Morning and afternoon registration carry overtones of 'thou shalt not be late'. There is a third possible type, namely expiatory rituals. These seem rare in schools, but an example occurs when a whole class is made to stay in after school to expiate some communal transgression.

All rituals play an important part in the social control of any school and in teaching to the pupils the norms that will enable them to behave as responsible citizens in the future. This process is not too difficult to achieve in grammar schools where the pupils are fairly certain to enter the élite that establishes many of the important norms in society. But rituals with expressive significance become very important in the socialisation of children in secondary modern schools since they are not sponsored to enter the élite of society. Many values that stress their socially inferior position and to which the children and their parents may very well be averse, are taught, perhaps unconsciously, thereby ensuring a measure of social consensus in an inegalitarian society. It would be interesting to examine the part such rituals play in a comprehensive school and to discover whether teachers who come to this new type of school import rituals from other types of school and thereby build processes into the school that offset the egalitarian aims implicit in the idea of a common school.

ORGANISATIONAL CULTURES

Within these organisational frameworks, and governed by the images of the various types of school that are held by those in the relevant organisation-set, there evolve very different cultures, that is, different systems of values and associated patterns of behaviour. The culture of the academic grammar school may be compared with that of the examination stream of the secondary modern school. Or the youth culture of the modern school may be contrasted with that of the bottom stream of a large grammar school.

These cultures do not really exist as such, but are constructs, abstracted from reality in a number of schools, that enable us to analyse these schools in an endeavour to see some social patterns in institutions with many differences. In the USA the academic culture has also been called 'college press' to indicate the instrumental dimension of pressure to reach college (university). The point that must be made is that there are different dimensions of such pressure. Some schools stress entry to the older English universities; others aim for local institutions. In grammar schools, the character of the sixth form differs and this flavours the academic culture of the whole school. The stress may be classical, scientific or technological. In other words, the academic culture is seen to be multidimensional.

There is conflicting evidence as to whether it is the most influential or the most numerous group that establishes the overall culture of the school. One study of a well known girls' college in the USA indicates that the very liberal values for which this institution was famous and which most of the students saw as marking its true culture were not in fact held by the majority of the young women who were its members. On the other hand an investigation of a number of high schools in the USA found that the particular branch of the youth culture that was named 'the fun sub-culture' was the most influential in these schools and was also that to which the majority of pupils subscribed.[3]

Where a school can establish a culture that comes to be held by the majority of its pupils, it is also very often able to define the desirable leisure time activities of these pupils. Here the school is not merely concentrating on extending its 'scope', that is widening the number of activities that its pupils undertake together, but it is trying to increase its 'pervasiveness'. The grammar school, for example, hopes that its pupils will attend school games fixtures, societies, concerts and plays, and that as a result the values implicit in this behaviour will have a wide influence so that these adolescents will follow similar interests in the holidays and, eventually, after they leave school.

There is, however, an important differentiating condition built into the grammar school. To enter a selective secondary school a child must, almost by definition, have been a 'best pupil' at his primary school. Yet there are not enough positions in any school class for all to attain this role in their new school, regardless of whether or not it is streamed. When this fact becomes clear to those pupils who are not in the top part of their class, there will be the temptation to create another role to give them some of the status that they have lost and this new role may turn out to be a deviant one. This process will be considered further in the next chapter, but it is worth pointing out that recruitment is important in this context. The greater the selectivity that can be exercised at the point of entry to the secondary school, the surer it is of excluding potential deviants who will oppose its academic aims. Thus, the degree of selection will influence the problems of disciplinary control in the grammar school and, possibly, inversely in the residual school since greater selectivity for the grammar school could create more problems in the modern school.

The second culture to which reference has been made, the youth culture, is another construct which must be justified by its usefulness in analysis. This culture is seen as a pattern of behaviour to which most adolescents conform in a fairly solid way. It is marked by values that are supposedly very different from those held in the adult world, since it is based on the overriding importance of such leisure activities as pop music, dancing and entertainment. However, the various studies that have been done in the USA have by no means established that this culture is characterised by absolute solidarity and conformity. Furthermore, the values centring on the world of entertainment are, under contemporary social conditions, also rated very highly by adults. Thus, the youth culture may be as much a distorted reflection of the adult world as a specific creation of youth itself.

A recent report of research illustrates the empirical results of applying the constructs of the academic and the youth cultures to a Lancashire secondary modern school for boys (Hargreaves, 16). The fifteen-year-olds were split into four streams and three recognisably different cultures could be constructed for analysing the whole of this age group in this school. There was, firstly, the A stream whose culture could be called academic. The boys in this stream gave high status to those who did well in school work, so that homework was important and bad behaviour was condemned. These boys, therefore, approved of briefcases in which to carry books home, were keen to wear the school tie and blazer, and were willing to have their hair cut short in the approved fashion. These manifest signs came to symbolise in ritual fashion their attachment to the academic culture.

In direct opposition to this pattern of behaviour was that of the D and most of the C streams who 'messed' rather than did any school work and who refused to wear the school uniform, instead adopting their own symbolic uniform of jeans together with long hair. For these boys in the anti-academic culture, the approved rewards of the school had become punishments. Thus, promotion to a higher stream for good work was felt as a punishment, since its effect would be to part a boy from his friends. Again, the normal punishment of a severe reprimand for bad work or scruffy dressing was a reward, since it drew attention to the boy concerned, thereby confirming or even increasing his status in his group.

The B stream was non-academic rather than anti-academic.

These boys aimed to have fun rather than 'mess'; they did not want to work too hard, but saw the connection between school and their future job, and wished to ensure that their school career led to a reasonable position. Neither their pattern of behaviour nor the visible signs of their culture were so obvious as in the other two cases. The analysis of the cultures in this particular school points very clearly to the central place of rewards and punishments in organisations and hence raises the problem of power in schools.

POWER

In a school, power is exerted by the head over his staff, by members of staff on other teachers, by teachers over the pupils and by pupils over other pupils. Those teachers and pupils who exert power have resources which they use to gain or wield power, and they may follow different styles in so doing. Thus a head may use a charismatic style to increase the great power that, in Britain, is traditionally a part of his position, but the ultimate climate of power may be very open since the head may not be in any way aloof. His style may be very friendly with little or no overt control or direction; finally, he may be paternal or even act like a martinet so as to evolve a closed style of power.[4]

Power is used in the formal decision-making process of the school. Often, such decisions will be made publicly in staff meetings. At other times, the head will give orders to the deputy head, to heads of departments and to those responsible for games or other school activities. Those who fill these positions will interpret the orders to those teachers under them. The lines of power in many institutions are laid out clearly so all know where the responsibility for taking a particular decision lies. Yet, particularly when a head sets a more open style in his use of power, decision-making can be diffused throughout the organisation. In schools where the rules about power are less fixed, change can be met more easily. The teacher on the spot can interpret school rules to meet a new infringement and speak to the head later about the particular problem.

It might be felt that where the degree of bureaucratisation is high in a school or in a school system the teachers would tend to feel a great loss of power. Yet evidence from the USA shows that this is apparently not the case.[5] It would seem that either of two processes are at work to prevent a feeling of powerlessness. Teachers may be differentially recruited to schools or school systems so that they can wield the amount of power that they desire, that is so that those who opt, whether consciously or not, for closed systems feel no loss of power. Or teachers may be recruited to posts where they have little power and then be socialised into acceptance of this as the norm.

The power of teachers over pupils is obvious in all schools. Power leads to COMPLIANCE and this has been categorised by Etzioni (11) under three general headings which may be applied usefully to power in schools. Firstly, there is compliance gained through such coercion as corporal punishment or a system of detentions. Control in the past rested very largely on coercive measures; compliance was exchanged by the pupils for freedom from punishment. Today Etzioni's two other categories are growing more relevant for the analysis of schools. Normative compliance depends upon socialising the pupils into the norms of the school, more particularly upon inducing them to take on the role of good pupil; this will be considered in the next chapter. Utilitarian compliance is also of greater importance today; this refers to the power of the school to provide useful services that may be withheld. Thus, success in examinations is made available and teachers can point out to erring pupils that by their misbehaviour they are endangering their chances of a good job on leaving school. Compliance of this utilitarian type may have been at work in the A stream of the secondary modern school to which reference was made in the last section. In much the same way the boys in the B stream realised that the teachers had some power over their future since they could supply or withhold references to potential employers.

One famous sociological analysis saw the school as existing in a constant state of perilous equilibrium based on a balance of power (Waller, 28). Compliance was achieved as exchanges of power resources took place between those in, and connected with, any school. Pupils exchanged good behaviour for adequate teaching, freedom from sarcasm or other more usual punishments such as writing lines or being caned. Similarly, teachers received freedom to teach as they thought best, for instance to choose their own text-books as long as the LEA were guaranteed a high pass rate in external examinations in return. The old boys' association of a school might donate the money for a swimming bath provided that the school promised not to alter its present image too drastically.

Such exchanges are complicated by the varying definitions of authority held by different teachers. An experienced secondary teacher knows that a class that comes to him after being taught by a colleague who is either a much stricter or a much laxer disciplinarian than he is will experience difficulty in settling down to the new definition of authority. Furthermore, ideas of authority change through time. Normative compliance is given more stress by contemporary educational theory than is coercion. However, there is the possibility that the most potent means of ensuring control in a large number of schools today is not recognised by many teachers. Utilitarian compliance may be very important for children who are studying for examinations, though reliance on this type of authority may not be welcome to teachers who stress the ultimate ends of education rather than such means as examinations.

A different type of control may be needed in schools where the youth culture predominates. Compliance in the case of children who are not working for examinations must be based on a different form of bargain between teacher and pupil. This has to be found within the range of values shared by teacher and pupil. So the teacher of English will use material drawn from the pop culture to initiate his pupils into the spirit of discrimination at which he aims; the teacher of Physical Education can use games to train his pupils, especially the boys, in the skills that he feels important. Such control has been called therapeutic (Bernstein, 31).

Many of the organisational changes that are suggested with the aim of increasing the influence of the large urban school over contemporary adolescents depend upon the creation of new positions, where the chances of conflict with pupils are as low as in the case of the Physical Education teacher. For example, welfare workers and counsellors are now appointed to some schools.

Though this development will increase the trend towards bureaucratisation, the role of those who fill these positions is to work to decrease the dangers implicit in the trend towards bureaucratisation and, at the same time, to help to create a more unitary culture within their schools.

SUMMARY

The images of schools that exist in the minds of the members of a society at any time are influenced by the historical development of these schools. In turn, these images influence the views of parents and of those in other organisations that interact with the schools. Such images also influence the ways in which those within the schools organise their schools as bureaucracies. Positions are created to which staff and pupils are allocated according to agreed criteria. This continuous process of allocation is deeply affected by the goals given to the organisation which can even influence such seemingly mundane matters as the colour of the classroom walls or the arrangement of the timetable. One important aspect of the organisation of any school is the way in which rituals are used to transmit values to the pupils. Ritual pervades schools and has both unifying and differentiating functions, but it plays a crucial part in providing social control, both in the present while pupils are at school and in the future when these children will be adults who, it is hoped, will form a cohesive society.

Within these organisations cultures grow up which differ by type of school and which may be in opposition to the goals sought by the school. The academic and adolescent cultures are contemporary conceptualisations of this fact. Teachers use the resources of power that they have in an exchange process to try to achieve their goals. Compliance is, however, rarely complete or permanent, since pupils, especially as they grow older, also have resources for power. Teachers try to achieve compliance in different ways according to the nature of their clients. Very often they are driven to employ utilitarian or even coercive measures when ideally they would prefer to use normative means to achieve their goals.

NOTES

1. Wheeler, S. 'The Structure of Formally Organized Socialization Settings', in Brim, O. G. & Wheeler, S. *Socialization after Childhood* (Wiley 1966, p. 89).

2. Kemeny, P. J. *The Technical School Leaver* (unpublished M.A. thesis, University of Sheffield, 1966); Holly, D. N. 'Profiting from the Comprehensive School', *British Journal of Sociology*, **16** (2) (June 1965).

3. Newcomb, T. H. *Personality and Social Change*, Holt, Rinehart and Winston 1943 (reprinted 1958); Coleman, J. S. *The Adolescent Society* (Basic Books 1961).

4. For these and other climates of power see Halpin, A. *Theory and Research in Administration* (New York, Macmillan 1966, especially pp. 174–181).

5. Moeller, G. H. & Charters, W. W. 'The Relationship of Bureaucratisation to Sense of Power among Teachers', *Administrative Science Quarterly*, **10** (4) (March 1966).

FURTHER READING

Barker and Gump (4). This account of empirical research shows the way size can influence the organisation of schools.

Bernstein, Elvin, & Peters (31). A theoretical paper of great sociological interest in which Durkheim's ideas on ritual are used to analyse contemporary developments in the organisation of various types of British school.

Blyth (6). Vol. II, chapter II, 'Three Traditions in English Primary Education', documents the main images of English primary schools and gives very full references.

Dahlke (10). Part III, 'Structure and Organization of the School', traces how school buildings (chapter 6), curricula (chapters 7 and 8), teaching methods (chapter 9) and rules (chapters 10–12) are all influenced by social values.

Etzioni (11). This is an introduction to organisation theory and in chapter 6, 'Organizational Control and Leadership', Etzioni gives his analysis of power and control.

Hargreaves (16). The whole book, an account of empirical research in a secondary modern school, leads to chapter 8, 'Two subcultures', which is very relevant to the point being made in the text.

Mead (21). This short book provides a stimulating account of images of schools in the USA and indicates the methods by which a similar account might be written for Britain.

Taylor (27). The whole book is relevant, but especially note chapter III, 'Parity of Esteem', for an analysis of how social forces altered the image of the secondary modern school that educationalists wished to create.

Waller (28). A classic on the sociology of the school, written in the '30s, but still well worth reading. In Part Four, 'The Teacher-Pupil Relationship', Waller describes some of the important social processes at work in the school.

7 The School Class

The goals given to an educational system, and the values implicit in them, penetrate right down to the classroom where the teacher interprets them in the lessons that he gives to his pupils. These abstract concepts help to govern the definition by the teacher of that demeanour which he considers acceptable. This role of 'good pupil' is offered to the child under circumstances in which great power can be brought to bear on him. Yet the role is not always taken, as has been seen in those situations where a strong anti-culture has become established.

THE GOOD PUPIL ROLE

In his theoretical analysis of the classroom, Parsons (36) has pointed out that teachers judge behaviour in school by two criteria, those of academic and moral achievement. The weight given to these criteria will vary with the goals and the clients of the school. Let us first consider the academic criterion. Here various types of intellectual attainment are at issue. The index used for measurement may be the number of passes in an external examination or the marks gained for a specific piece of class work. Such attainments may, however, be of less importance if a teacher wishes to judge a pupil merely by his intelligence when he may quote the child's score on one of the many intelligence tests. In some cases, the particular attainment given priority may be social rather than intellectual; current standards of good manners are often rated high in schools, particularly in the case of girls.

However, social behaviour is usually judged by moral criteria and considered to be the result of moulding personality or, to use the rather emotive British phrase, 'forming character'. Yet the success of such moral education is judged by the outward and visible signs of its inner presence. Academic attainment demands the ability to defer the immediate gratification of many childish or adolescent wants and pleasures; teachers tend to judge 'strong character' by such behaviour as doing homework instead of dating a girl-friend or staying on into the sixth form instead of taking a job with the chance to earn enough money to own a high-powered motor cycle. Good pupils remain subordinate to the school. Thus, acts that indicate allegiance to the teenage culture are used by teachers to judge how far a pupil is departing from the role of good pupil.

Such indices are used as how the pupil dresses, how long his hair is, whether she uses make-up or wears a tight skirt and blouse.[1] A very important influence on the content of the good pupil role is the way in which 'precocity' is defined. This role, like all roles, has a range of tolerated behaviour, but for each age of pupil some level of academic performance and moral behaviour is considered advanced enough to be called precocious and as a result the child who exceeds these norms will be called an exceptional pupil. In the case of academic achievement, his behaviour will earn rewards from his teachers, though his peers may call him a 'swot'. But the reverse may be true of moral precocity, where his teacher's reprimand may be offset by the approval of his peers. The sanctions of reward and punishment are used by staff to attempt to force the pupil to take the role desired.

Deviance will be punished with varying success. The behaviour considered by the teacher as deviant will vary with the nature of his clients. The grammar school teacher will excuse behaviour in a working class child that he would condemn in a pupil from a middle class home and the teacher in a secondary modern school would expect less from those of his pupils that came from 'bad homes'. The oft-used phrase 'he should have known better' indicates that a double standard of good pupil may be at work. Similarly, the teacher will use a dual standard to judge the same morally offensive action; in the case of a working class child it will be blamed on a poor environment, whereas in a middle class child the behaviour may be considered the result of independence born of high intelligence or perhaps learned in a bohemian atmosphere.[2]

Very docile children or those in poor health are just as likely to be labelled deviant as those who are thought of as behaving badly. One of the dangers of this process is that such pupils can be confirmed as permanent deviants. The best example is the process whereby a child is made a scapegoat. His fellow pupils may bring this about by teasing him. Because of their youth they do not know what they are doing. However, teachers who should be aware of this possible effect may label a child as a deviant in such a way that he becomes the scapegoat of both the teacher and the class. The child may be cast in this role for much of his school career with harmful effects on the development of his personality.

Children are not only pupils. They play many other roles and bring some important latent roles into the school. Their sex role is crucial in this respect. It seems easier in our culture for girls to play the good pupil role than it is for boys; in primary school there are more girls than boys in the streams for those of high ability.[3] By the criterion of moral achievement, girls also do better than boys, since their rate of juvenile delinquency is lower. Age is another powerful latent role; clearly, the potential power of a pupil rises as he grows older and less dependent upon his elders. Social class is perhaps the latent role upon which most research has been done. It has been shown that children from different social classes bring to the role of pupil different values, different modes of thought and different perceptions of the school situation. Different neighbourhoods have 'contextual effects' on the child; in some areas the child comes to school rating one type of achievement high, perhaps verbal achievement, whereas a second child from another part of the same school catchment area may have learnt to stress achievement with his hands.[4] In addition to these rather subtle latent roles there are more obvious and often purely physical, roles that influence the way that a child behaves as a pupil. Such are ethnic roles; the children of immigrants bring many of the values implicit in the culture of their parents' homeland to the schools of their adopted country.

Finally, physically handicapped, or even fat, children bring a stigma to their attempts to play the good pupil role. To a large extent, it is the power of such latent roles that prevents the school from achieving complete success in teaching all to be good pupils as it defines that role.

Those who are successful are rewarded in various ways. As a result of the continuous assessment by teachers of their academic and moral achievement, pupils are made prefects, form captains or given some position of responsibility for an extracurricular activity. Success at games, if accompanied by a measure of moral achievement, may be rewarded by appointment as a team captain. Sometimes such positions are awarded through election by one's peers, in which case the criteria of assessment may differ somewhat from those used by the staff. Some positions in schools are also available as rewards to 'willing workers'.[5] Children without great talent, but who persevere and have a deep interest in some activity, may be rewarded by appointment to the committee of a school society or to such a post as assistant librarian. In most schools there are enough positions that demand a variety of qualities to reward the diverse personalities of the pupils.

CLASSROOM POSITIONS

The normative isolation of any teacher in his classroom tends to ensure that his work remains largely hidden from public view and hence he has the chance to structure the positions that he makes available in his class, largely in the manner that he wishes. Yet he is constrained by many influences. The goals of the school govern his teaching. A teacher in an academic school will create one set of positions with associated role expectations, while one whose aim, like many urban secondary modern schools, is mainly custodial, will create another set. The nature of the task of teaching can be influenced by such goals as that of egalitarianism which may determine the composition of the groupings in the school. Such groups may be undifferentiated by sex or ability so that the teacher must structure the positions available in a different way from the way he could do in an élitist or single sex school where more homogeneous groups are possible. The writing and casting of a class play illustrates the point, since those available to act will determine the positions created. There can be no parts for girls or several, all the parts may have few lines or some may be longer if more able children are available to fill them.

Goals are also important in determining whether or not monitors are created in a class and in deciding how long such positions are to be held by any one child. In egalitarian schools, if monitors are created, the positions tend to be rotated weekly or monthly so that all have a chance to fill them. In élitist schools, on the other hand, monitors are much more common and the positions tend to be held by one incumbent for a whole term or even a year.

Factors involved in the teaching of a subject can also be important: a geometry lesson often demands the distribution of equipment that is potentially very dangerous in some children's hands, whereas in most English lessons such a problem does not arise. The size of the groupings within the class can also be varied by the class teacher. Large groups increase the resources of each individual group, but they alter the role of those within the group, since greater size works to reduce the chances available to each child to use his resources to the maximum.

POWER

Whether or not the children in a class learn the good pupil role depends greatly on the resources for power that are available to the teacher and on how he uses them. The power of any teacher is partly inherent in his position and partly dependent on how charismatic a person he himself is. From an organisational standpoint, what is important is to isolate just which parts of the teacher's behaviour is seen by his pupils as exerting power. A recent report found that children of primary school age perceived four main categories of power amongst their peers.[6] The intention here is to use these same categories to examine power relationships between pupils and teachers.

First, a 'smart' teacher or one who has 'good ideas about how to make fun' can influence his pupils' behaviour; in other words expertness in material and method is a resource for power. It is arguable whether the image of the teacher as an expert is as potent in the field of morals as it is in academic or other matters pertaining to school. Secondly, children appear to obey a 'strong' teacher; this finding confirms the point in the last chapter that coercion can lead to compliance. Thirdly, children tend to do what a 'friendly' teacher tells them; there is a group of social-emotional resources that can be used, though which of these an individual teacher can deploy may depend largely on his own personality. The role around which a teacher has come to organise his own identity will influence how he acts; thus, a teacher who sees herself as a mother-figure will more easily use social-emotional power than one who has taken up a more withdrawn stance to life. Lastly, a teacher who 'plays with you a lot' and seems a near-equal, influences his pupils; this may be termed an associational resource. Very often such expressive authority over pupils depends upon their perceiving the teacher to have achieved something of an instrumental nature; for instance, a popular man teacher may be a good athlete.

In addition, a number of other unclassifiable sources of power were found. For example, a teacher who is 'nice-looking' can have great power over some pupils. This last case illustrates clearly the general point that pupils of different age and sex will give these categories differing weight and also will not react in the same way to each type of power when used by teachers of different age and sex. Thus, the power of a woman teacher over a girl who has a crush on her is only available within a limited age range in both teacher and pupil.

The way in which a teacher uses these categories of power as sanctions against his pupils is an important determinant of his success. The teaching methods that he chooses stress various categories of his power. He may be a traditional teacher who tends to lecture in a dominant manner and often uses coercion or he may give the children considerable freedom, relying on associational or emotional resources to control his class. He may use the 'witch-hunt' syndrome against deviants.[7] Here, the teacher exchanges his approval for the help of his class against a pupil who is not achieving the academic or moral norm of the class. The children are encouraged to compete for their teacher's approval in pointing out in public to a classmate his errors and misbehaviour.

The various positions that are available in the classroom can be used as a resource for power in exchange for compliance. Mention has already been made of the way in which such positions of responsibility as that of monitor can be given to a good pupil as a reward for attainment. In addition, purely geographical positions in the classroom itself are important. Friends can be allowed to sit together or, if they talk too much, can be separated. Seats near to windows or radiators can be used in a similar way. Likewise, places at the back of the room may be given to those who work hard and those at the front to those who need supervision.

The type of tests of academic attainment and the way in which they are applied influences the nature of the rewards available to the teacher to exchange for attainment. Tests based on multi-choice questions encourage pupils to stress details, examinations made up of essay-type questions lead to an emphasis on structure. Continuous assessment by weekly tests creates an atmosphere of nervous tension; striving to gain rewards or to avoid punishment becomes the norm (Henry, 17). Internally assessed examinations of the type now permissible in the English Certificate of Secondary Education will result in a different power exchange than in the case where pupils sit such external examinations as the General Certificate of Education. In the latter case pupil and teacher will tend to gang up on their mutual enemy, the external examiner, for example, by trying to forecast questions. In the former case, however, the pupil will be suspicious of his teacher, since he will find himself in role-conflict, not knowing whether his teacher is friend or foe.[8]

These ways of using power will bring about various social climates in the classroom. One method of analysing these different results would be to discuss them in terms of morale, in much the same way as methods of wage payment are related to industrial productivity. This could be as misleading in the case of the school as it is for factories. Morale and productivity are not necessarily directly related. If a teacher's goal is a high pass rate in an external examination, the morale of his class may be very low, since his pupils may hate the hard work that is forced upon them. On the other hand, the teacher may aim to have a very relaxed class and may refrain from pressing his pupils to work. In the first case, productivity may be high and morale low, in the second, productivity may be low and morale high.

The process of teaching almost inevitably leads to a clash between the teacher and the learner because mistakes of both a moral and an academic nature are seen to occur. The really difficult problems in the use of power happen when there are children in the class whose norms vary greatly from those of their teacher. In these cases, often the school cannot rely on a measure of social control due to normative socialisation that is supported by the influence of the home. This is especially the case in problem urban areas where parents give little support to the school. In all cases where misbehaviour or academic failure takes place, both the child and the teacher are threatened. Both must act to confirm their identities, the teacher to restore his authority and the pupil to regain his lost status. But in a class where a strong anticulture exists the result of a teacher using his power to punish may be a further loss of status that incites the pupil to redeem his lost status by another misdemeanour. The exact way in which a teacher tells a pupil to desist can influence this process. Clarity in defining the deviant act, providing it is not overdone, shows the child the boundaries of good and bad behaviour. Firmness is important, but it may pass over into roughness.[9] This may lead to the child feeling that he has been labelled as a bad pupil rather than that he has been helped to become a good one.

In this situation, the ultimate effect of the teacher's attempts to gain compliance is that he comes to feel that the achieving of his goals is impossible. One or more of his class has come to be labelled as deviant and now plays, probably with some pride, the bad pupil role. In the Lancashire secondary modern school for boys to which reference has already been made, the pupils of the *C* and *D* streams bore this label and confirmed themselves in this role by further deviant acts. For these adolescents, high status was associated with a court record and with petty theft. There was in these classes a central core of deviants; the main criterion for membership was success at fighting (Hargreaves, 16).

DIVISIVE PROCESSES

There are two divisive processes at work within the organisation of the school (Lacey, 34). The first to be considered is the process whereby children become differentiated from one another in their school classes. On entry to the primary school, the children form one group; the main differences that are visible either to the teacher or the pupils themselves are based on physical characteristics. However, very soon they become known to each other by such distinctions as being good at school work or bad at games. Stars are given and marks awarded for academic achievement, lists of the numbers of stars gained by each pupil are posted for all the class to see and for parents to read on open nights. Even in unstreamed schools groups that are differentiated are found within each class. The pupils soon know which groups are considered good and which bad, often because the teacher draws invidious comparisons between the groups, such as 'Surely Mary's group can do better than Fiona's?' or 'Well, that's a good effort for Ian's group'.

By the time that the children move to secondary school some have come to be labelled as good pupils. There is a growing body of evidence in the USA to show that as a result of this process children come to hold a good or a bad self-concept of their own academic (or moral) ability, even in such specific subjects as English or Mathematics.[10] This self-concept has a strong influence on whether or not they have high attainments in school. In other words, the process of labelling acts as a self-fulfilling prophecy. In British schools, streaming by ability reinforces the way in which the process works within individual classes.

Those who achieve a place in a selective secondary school or a high stream in a streamed comprehensive school have almost always been good pupils in their primary schools. When they enter their new schools, all these children are mixed together in a new class so that it is impossible for all to continue to play their former role. Some must be disappointed. They no longer receive rewarding experiences and have high status in the eyes of their teacher or their peers. Children in their first year at secondary school may not be affected in this way, but by their second year a change takes place and the second process, namely that of polarisation, begins to work. Gradually, an anti-culture is evolved. The failure of those who achieve low academic results becomes visible to all and since status, particularly in selective secondary schools, is related closely to this criterion, those at the bottom of the class try to regain status by other methods. This often means by clowning. The almost inevitable result is that a group becomes labelled as anti-academic and badly behaved.

In the secondary modern school, this process is the more powerful since the pupils there have failed twice, both in not gaining a place at grammar school and again in their present efforts in their lower status secondary school. Ironically, promotion between streams, supposedly a reward for a good pupil, can be detrimental to those children who can only just hold their places in the higher stream. The best pupil in the B stream may fail to be even an average pupil in the A stream and join those who have polarised out as the deviant group at the bottom of the higher class. The pupils themselves support the workings of these two processes since they come to have stereotypes of each other as A types ('brainy') or B types ('clots'). This hostility, like all fixed ideas, is very hard to remove. One way to change this attitude is to create situations where the children mix together in some purposeful activity. The normal secondary school timetable prevents this as classes move round *en bloc*. Hence, mixing is only possible in such extra-curricular activities as in playing games or the meetings of societies. Here, children can appreciate each other's real, rather than imaginary, qualities. We thus reach the unexpected conclusion that games and societies, introduced into British schools for the purpose of 'character building', have a part to play in breaking down the forces at work that help to check the full development of intellectual ability.

In connection with this last point, the argument is often used that success on the playing field is used as a compensation by those who fail in the classroom. Research done in London and North West England in secondary schools of all types, selective and non-selective, coeducational and single-sex, has examined this issue and found that the compensation thesis seems untrue.[11] Members of academic streams were over- rather than underrepresented in the school teams considered, the one possible exception may be among children in B streams in four stream schools.

SUMMARY

At school, children are called upon to play the good pupil role which is based on academic and moral criteria. In British schools, where the pastoral tradition is rated high, much stress is put on the latter criterion and hence attention is given to 'character building'. Sanctions are brought to bear on pupils, but children bring latent roles into the school that may hinder their acceptance of the role of good pupil. Those who are judged to succeed are allocated to the positions that the school sees as having prestige. Teachers create positions in their classrooms in accordance with their own goals and use their power to try to make their pupils play the good pupil role as they define it. Different styles of teaching affect the success or otherwise of their efforts; even such an apparently purely administrative matter as the modes of examining can influence the social climate of the classroom. Deviance is almost inevitable in any situation where teaching occurs, but it can be reinforced if teachers label the deviant as such. There are, in addition, divisive processes at work in many classrooms, especially around the time of transfer to secondary school, that may create deviants.

NOTES

1. See Sugarman, B. 'Involvement in youth culture, academic achievement, and conformity in school: an empirical study of London schoolboys', *British Journal of Sociology,* **18** (2) (June 1967).
2. Becker, H. S. 'Social Class Variations in the Teacher-Pupil Relationship', *Journal of Educational Sociology*, **27** (April 1952).
3. *Children in Their Primary Schools*, Vol. II (H.M.S.O. p. 551).
4. Boocock, S. S. 'Towards a Sociology of Learning', *Sociology of Education,* **39** (1) (Winter 1966).
5. Jones, M. C. 'A Study of Socialisation Patterns at the High School Level', *Journal of Genetic Psychology*, **93** (1st half) (September 1958).
6. Gold, M. 'Power in the Classroom', *Sociometry,* **21** (1) (March 1958).

7. Henry J. 'Attitude Organisation in Elementary School Classrooms' in Spindler, G. D. *Education and Culture* (Holt, Rinehart and Winston 1965).

8. I owe much of this paragraph to remarks made on several occasions by Professor W. Taylor of Bristol.

9. Kounin, J. S., Gump, P. V. & Ryan, J. J. 'Explorations in classroom management', *Journal of Teacher Education*, **12** (2) (June 1961).

10. Brookover, W. B., Thomas, S. & Paterson, A. 'Self-Concept of Ability and School Achievement', *Sociology of Education*, 37 (3) (Spring 1964).

11. Start, K. B. 'Substitution of games performance for academic achievement as a measure of achieving status among secondary school children', *British Journal of Sociology*, **17** (3) (September 1966).

FURTHER READING

Hargreaves (16). This book is just as relevant to this chapter on the school class as it was to the last chapter on the school as a whole.

Henry (17). Chapter 8, 'Golden Rule Days: American Schoolrooms', indicates the type of exchange process that can take place between teacher and pupil, and its possible effects on the pupil's personality.

Lacey (34). This report of empirical research in the first two classes of a boys' grammar school develops a theoretical sociological model to explain important processes at work in such a school situation.

Parsons (36). In this theoretical paper the American school class, mainly at primary level, is analysed as a social system. The framework developed is very relevant to British schools.

Postscript

In this book we have seen how the goals given to the British educational system govern the organisation of the various types of school that are brought into being. The nature of the roles of the staff and pupils has been examined and an indication given of the way in which the academic and moral outcomes of this system are assessed. Possibly the main general conclusion that can be drawn is that a pupil will achieve up to the academic and moral standards that are required of him if he feels that it is to his benefit to exchange these attainments for his other interests. If, for example, good marks are rewarded by his peers and by his teacher, or if wearing school uniform gains him a reference for a job, *and* if no latent role leads the pupil to believe that these particular attainments are impossible for him, then and only then will he exchange his compliance for what the teacher has to offer. The process is not automatic and many of the hindrances are sociological in nature. Some of the variables intervening in the learning process are determined by the larger social structure outside the school, but many are deeply rooted in the organisation of the school and in the face-to-face situation in the classroom itself. Appreciation of the important influence that the social structure has within the school is now more common. Much of what has been said in this book is a plea for the greater recognition of the second group of forces, namely those emanating from the social organisation of the school itself.

Bibliography

Books

1. Ashley, B. J., Cohen, H. & Slatter, R. G. *An Introduction to the Sociology of Education* (Macmillan, in the press)

2. Banks, O. *Parity and Prestige in English Secondary Education* (Routledge 1957)

3. Baron, G. & Tropp, A. *Teachers in England and America,* in Halsey, Floud & Anderson (14)

4. Barker, R. G. & Gump, P. V. *Big School, Small School* (Stanford, California 1964)

5. Bidwell, C. E. *The School as a Formal Organization*, in J. G. March (editor), Handbook of Organizations (Rand McNally 1965)

6. Blyth, W. A. L. *English Primary Education* (Routledge 1965)

7. Clark, B. R. *Educating the Expert Society* (Chandler 1962)

8. Corwin, R. G. *A Sociology of Education* (Appleton-Century-Crofts 1965)

9. Cruickshank, M. *Church and State in Education* (Macmillan 1963)

10. Dahlke, O. H. *Values in Culture and Classroom* (Harper 1958)

11. Etzioni, A. *Modern Organizations* (Prentice-Hall 1964)

12. Floud, J. E. & Scott, W. *Recruitment to Teaching in England and Wales,* in Halsey, Floud & Anderson (14)

13. Halpin, A. W. *Theory and Research in Administration* (New York, Macmillan 1966)

14. Halsey, A. H., Floud, J. E. & Anderson, C. A. *Education, Economy and Society* (Free Press 1961)

15. Hans, N. *New Trends in Education in the Eighteenth Century* (Routledge 1951)

16. Hargreaves, D. H. *Social Relations in a Secondary School* (Routledge 1967)

17. Henry, J. *Culture Against Man* (Random House 1963)

18. Herriott, R. E. & St. John, N. H. *Social Class and the Urban School* (Wiley 1966)

19. Lester Smith, W. O. *Education* (Pelican 1957)

20. Lester Smith, W. O. *Government of Education* (Pelican 1965)

21. Mead, M. *The School in American Culture* (Harvard 1951); also in Halsey, Floud & Anderson (14)

22. Musgrave, P. W. *The Sociology of Education* (Methuen 1965)

23. Musgrave, P. W. *Technical Change, the Labour Force and Education* (Pergamon 1967)

24. Musgrave, P. W. *Society and Education in England since 1800* (Methuen 1968)

25. Osborne, G. S. *English and Scottish Schools* (Longmans 1967)

26. Plowden Report *Children and their Primary Schools*, Vol. II, Appendix 13 (HMSO 1967)

27. Taylor, W. *The Secondary Modern School* (Faber 1963)

28. Waller, W. *The Sociology of Teaching* (Wiley 1933); reprinted Russell & Russell 1961

29. Weinberg, I. *The English Public School* (Atherton Press 1967)

Articles

30. Baron, G. 'Some Aspects of the Headmaster Tradition', *Leeds Research and Studies*, No. 14 (June 1956)

31. Bernstein, B., Elvin, H. L. & Peters, R. S. 'Ritual in Education', *Philosophical Transactions of the Royal Society of London*, Series B (Biological Sciences 1966)

32. Finlayson, D. S. & Cohen, L. 'The Teacher's Role: A Comparative Study of College of Education Students and Head Teachers', *British Journal of Educational Psychology*, **37** (2) (February 1967)

33. Hoyle, E. H. 'Organisational Analysis in the Field of Education', *Educational Research*, **3** (2) (February 1965)

34. Lacey, C. 'Some sociological concomitants of academic streaming in a grammar school', *British Journal of Sociology*, **17** (3) (September 1966)

35. Musgrove, F. & Taylor P. H. 'Teachers' and Parents' Conceptions of the Teacher's Role', *British Journal of Educational Psychology*, **35** (2) (June 1965)

36. Parsons, T. 'The School as a Social System', *Harvard Education Review*, **29** (Fall 1959); also in Halsey, Floud & Anderson (14)

37. Taylor, W. 'The Training College Principal', *Sociological Review*, **12** (2) (New Series) (July 1964)

38. Turner, R. H. 'Sponsored and Contest Mobility in the School System', *American Sociological Review*, **25** (5) (December 1960); also in Halsey, Floud & Anderson (14)

39. Westwood, L. J. 'The Role of the Teacher', I and II, *Educational Research*, **9** (2) (February 1967) and **10** (1) (November 1967)

40. Wilson, B. R. 'The Teacher's Role', *British Journal of Sociology*, **13** (1) (March 1962)

Glossary

AUTHORITY. The socially recognised right to exercise power (*qv*). May be based on coercion, tradition or charisma (*qv*), or a mixture of these.

BUREAUCRACY. A particular type of organisation (*qv*), marked by a formal hierarchy and a set of rules governing authority (*qv*) and procedure.

CHARISMA. Power of leadership or authority (*qv*) based on the exceptional or unusual qualities of a leader, e.g. a particular type of personality.

DIFFERENTIATE. The process whereby a whole, e.g. a role, splits into separate parts, often having highly specialised functions.

EXPRESSIVE. Relating to behaviour that is concerned with maintaining the emotional balance of a group (*cf* instrumental (*qv*)).

IDEOLOGY. A pattern of beliefs and ideas which justify to those who hold it a certain social phenomenon, *e.g.* a political ideology. Often such patterns contain a strong element of rationalisation.

INSTRUMENTAL. Relating to behaviour that is directed to achieving a goal (*cf.* expressive (*qv*)).

NORM. A standard shared by a social group to which members are expected to conform. Such conformity is enforced by sanctions.

ORGANISATION. A social grouping, often very complex, formed to follow one or more specific goals.

POSITION. A place in a particular social structure.

PROBLEM. The way in which significant members of an organisation (*qv*) perceive its goal(s) at any given time (*cf.* task (*qv*)).

POWER. The capacity to control the action of others.

ROLE. The expected behaviour of the incumbent of a given social position (*qv*). Should be differentiated from role behaviour, or what the incumbent actually does.

ROLE-SET. The array of roles (*qv*) associated with other positions (*qv*) with which a role incumbent will come into contact as he plays his particular role.

SOCIALISATION. The process whereby members of social groups learn the roles expected of them within that group.

STATUS. The prestige given to any position (*qv*).

TASK. The goal(s) defined for an organisation (*qv*) (*cf.* problem (*qv*)).

TOTAL. The degree to which an organisation (*qv*) is cut off from its surrounding environment.

Index

administration, 23–8
Arnold, Thomas, 38, 39, 40, 49
Ashley, B. J., 9, 98
assembly, morning, 40–1, 49, 74
authority, 39, 47, 67, 70, 72, 74, 75, 81, 92, 100

Banks, O., 15, 22, 98
Barker, R. G., and Gump, P. V., 70, 83, 98
Baron, G., 38, 51, 99
Baron, G., and Tropp, A., 53, 66, 98
Becker, H. S., 66, 95
Bernstein, B., Elvin, H. L., and Peters, R. S., 74, 81, 83, 99
Bidwell, C. E., 9, 98
Bidwell, C. E., and Vreeland, R. S., 66
Blyth, W. A. L., 69, 83, 98
boarding schools, 38, 39, 41, 56, 70, 72, 75
Boards
  of Governors, 20, 27–8, 53
  of Managers, 20, 27–8, 53
  School, 12, 20, 26
Boocock, S. S., 95
Brim, O. G., and Wheeler, S., 83
Brookover, W. B., Thomas, S., and Paterson, A., 96
bureaucracy, 7, 26–7, 34, 39, 43, 46, 69–72, 79–80, 82, 100
Burnham, P. S., 50

careers, 45, 55, 60, 61, 63, 69–70
  masters, 49
Carlson, R. O., 36
Central Advisory Council, 33–4
chaplains, school, 49, 74
charisma, 39, 43, 50, 64, 79, 89, 100
Clark, Burton R., 27, 36, 98
class
  middle, 17, 35, 38, 39, 42, 58, 59, 63, 71, 72, 86–7
  social, 13–14, 16, 29, 48, 87
  working, 14, 33, 35, 42, 58, 59, 68, 69, 71, 86
classrooms, 49, 50, 54, 57, 62, 63, 64, 71, 72, 73, 85, 88–9, 91, 97
clients, 9, 21, 30, 35, 42, 44, 57–9, 61, 67, 68, 69
codes, 12, 17, 24, 29, 52
coeducation, 57, 73
coercion, 63–4, 80, 81, 90
Coleman, J. S., 83
colleges of education, 30–2, 40, 45, 59–60, 63
compliance, 80, 81, 90, 91, 92, 97
comprehensive schools, 15, 42, 44–5, 60, 61, 69, 70, 72, 73, 76, 93
conflict, 55, 58, 62, 72, 91, 92
control, 40, 56, 58, 72, 73, 75, 80, 81
corporal punishment, 64, 80, 81
Corwin, R. G., 27, 36, 98
Crowther (*15 to 18*) Report, 66
Cruickshank, M., 22, 98
cultures, 76–9, 82, 85, 86, 92, 94
curriculum, 13, 14–15, 18, 25, 33, 34, 40, 42–3, 49, 68, 73, 89

Dahlke, O. H., 73, 83, 98
Department of Education and Science (DES), 24–5, 26, 32
deputy head, 8, 38, 45, 79
  see also roles, deputy head
deviance, 77, 78, 86–7, 90, 92, 94
differentiation, 47, 55, 74, 77, 88, 93–5, 100
Director of Education, 26, 27

economy, the, 16–19, 24, 31, 39, 40, 53, 60
Education Acts
  England (1870), 11, 20, 25; (1902), 11, 20, 26, 31, 40; (1944), 11, 12, 15, 20, 26, 27, 29, 35, 52, 23, 68
  Scotland (1872), 12, 20, 25; (1918), 12, 26; (1945), 12, 15, 20, 26, 57, 29
Education Committee, 26, 27
egalitarianism, 13–16, 18, 24, 29, 31, 33, 35, 53, 68, 69, 73, 76, 88, 89
elementary schools, 11–12, 15, 16, 17, 19, 20, 31, 40, 45, 69
eleven-plus, 35, 53
élites, 13–16, 17, 29, 30, 68, 73, 75, 76, 88, 89

Etzioni, A., 36, 50, 66, 80, 83, 98
examinations, 13, 40, 41, 42, 53, 54, 60, 64, 66, 67, 71, 76, 80, 81, 85, 91
exchange processes, 41, 43, 44, 80–1, 90–1, 97
expressive, 42, 43, 44, 46, 47, 48, 57, 58, 61, 69, 75, 90, 100

Finlayson, D. S., and Cohen, L., 61, 63, 66, 99
Floud, J. E., and Scott, W., 59, 66, 98

games, 41, 52, 62, 64, 71, 73, 74, 77, 79, 81, 88, 93, 94–5
goals, 7, 8, 23, 29, 30, 38, 42, 43, 48, 55, 56, 69, 72, 73, 88, 89, 91, 92
  British educational system, 10–22, 24, 40, 67, 85, 97
  changing of, 33–5
  displacement of, 46, 65
Gold, M., 95
grammar schools, 14, 15, 20, 39, 40, 42, 44, 48, 60, 61, 68–9, 71, 73, 75, 76, 77, 86, 94

Halpin, A., 41, 51, 83, 98
Halsey, A. H., Floud, J. E., and Anderson, C. A., 98, 99
Hans, N., 17, 22, 98
Hargreaves, D. H., 78, 83, 92, 96, 98
head, the, 19, 20, 28, 38–46, 58, 61, 64, 70, 71, 74, 79
  see also roles, head
Headmasters' Conference (HMC), 40, 44
Henry, J., 91, 96, 98
Herriot, R. E., and St. John, N. H., 42, 51, 98
HMIs, *see* inspectors
Holly, D. N., 83
house system, 70, 71, 75
Hoyle, E. H., 9, 99

ideology, 17, 46, 100
  see also laissez-faire
independence, 18–21, 30, 32, 38, 40, 41, 42, 53, 72
infant schools, 42, 57, 61
inspectors (HMIs), 19, 24–5, 32, 34, 40, 54
instrumental, 42, 43, 46, 47, 48, 58, 90, 100

janitor, 49
Jones, M. C., 95

Kemeny, P. J., 83
Knox, John, 12, 13
Kounin, J. S., Gump, P. V., and Ryan, J. J., 96

labelling process, 87, 92, 93–4
labour force, the, 16, 18, 30, 35
Lacey, C., 93, 96, 99
laissez-faire, 11, 14, 16, 17, 19
  ideology of, 18, 24, 25, 39, 46
leadership, 43, 44, 48
Local Education Authorities (LEAs), 25–7, 28, 31, 34, 40, 41, 46, 68, 70, 81

Mead, M., 68, 83, 99
modern schools, 15–16, 35, 42, 48, 58, 60, 61, 68–9, 71, 75, 76, 77, 78, 80, 86, 88, 92, 94
Moeller, G. H., and Charters, W. W., 83
monitors, *see* prefects
Musgrave, P. W., 18, 22, 34, 60, 66, 99
Musgrove, F., and Taylor, P. H., 62, 66, 99

Newcomb, T. H., 83
Newsom Report (*Half Our Future*), 66
norms, 24, 31, 45, 48, 53, 57, 59, 64, 72, 74, 75, 80, 90, 92, 100

Osborne, G. S., 10, 22, 99

parent–teacher associations, 35, 42, 54, 68
parents, 21, 28, 30, 35, 42, 43, 54, 58, 62–3, 65, 69, 70, 76, 92
parochial schools, 12
Parsons, T., 85, 96, 99
pastoral responsibility, 39, 40, 49, 52, 53, 62, 64, 70, 74
Plowden Report (*Children and their Primary Schools*), 28, 36, 66, 95, 99
positions, 7, 24, 26, 34, 55, 61, 69, 71, 72, 73, 77, 79, 81, 88–9, 91, 100
power, 7, 43, 49, 54, 63, 64, 69, 70, 74, 79–82, 85, 87, 89–92, 100
prefects, 39, 58, 71, 72, 73, 74, 75, 88, 89, 91
primary schools, 20, 24, 27, 42, 45, 56, 57, 58, 60, 69, 72, 73, 75, 77, 89, 93
problem, 41, 42, 48, 100
profession, the teaching, 43, 55, 56, 59, 60, 63, 64
proprietary schools, 14, 18, 19
public schools, 14, 19, 20, 34, 38, 40, 61, 62

recruitment
  administrators, 24, 25, 26, 32, 33
  clients, 77
  governing bodies, 28
  heads, 27, 28, 39, 40, 44–6
  teachers, 48, 57, 59–61, 69, 80
references, character, 43, 44, 97

religion, 10–13, 28, 31, 41, 52
religious instruction, 12, 13, 53
ritual, 74–6, 78
role-set, 27, 40, 41, 46, 54, 61, 62, 68, 72, 100
roles, 8, 24, 26, 50, 100
  ancillary, 46–50, 64
  deputy head, 8, 38, 47–9
  good pupil, 77, 80, 85–8, 91, 92, 93
  head, 8, 38–46, 56
  latent, 56, 57–8, 63, 87–8, 97
  pupil, 73, 77, 89, 94, 97
  sex, 57, 75, 87, 90
  teacher, 8, 31, 34, 52–66, 72, 86, 89–92, 97

schools
  images of, 67–9, 81
  size of, 44, 45–7, 48–9, 55, 58, 70–1
  see also under specific types
Scotland
  administration, 24–8
  educational goals, 10–21
  heads, 39, 45
  schools, 12, 14, 44, 45, 68, 75
  teachers, 53, 54, 59, 69
  universities, 15, 18, 24, 30
Scottish Education Department (SED), 21, 24, 32
secondary schools, 15, 18, 19, 24, 27, 28, 30, 40, 44, 57, 58, 62, 93–5
selection, 15, 16, 69, 77
sixth form, 58, 61, 76, 86
Smith, W. O. Lester, 22, 36, 98
socialisation, 101
  children, 71, 75, 92
  teachers, 31, 45, 46, 63, 80
societies, school, 73, 77, 94
Start, K. B., 96
status, 101
  educational, 17, 54, 60
  individual, 41, 49, 69, 77, 78, 92, 93, 94
  social, 14, 29, 35, 59, 74
  teachers, 45, 52, 61
streaming, 42, 62, 73, 77, 78, 80, 92, 93, 94–5
Sugarman, B., 95

Task, 41, 42, 46, 68, 101
Taylor, W., 35, 37, 51, 69, 84, 96, 99
teachers
  English, 30
  salaries of, 17, 43, 60
  Scottish, 13, 30
  see also roles, teacher
teaching methods, 61–5, 87, 88–9, 90, 92
technical schools, 15, 35, 60, 71–2, 73
total, 56–7, 70, 71, 101
training colleges, *see* colleges of education
Treasury, the, 17, 23–4, 32
tripartite system, 15, 29, 30
Turner, R. H., 29, 37, 99
turnover of staff, 43, 58, 60

uniform, school, 75, 78, 97
universities, 24, 29, 31, 32–3, 58, 59, 61, 76
  English, 18
  Oxford and Cambridge, 13, 24, 44
  Scottish, 15, 18, 24, 30
  technological, 18
University Grants Committee (UGC), 32, 33
USA, 27, 41, 53, 54, 61, 68, 70, 76, 77, 78, 80, 93

Waller, W., 80, 84, 99
Weinberg, I., 44, 51, 99
Westwood, L. J., 61, 66, 99
Wheeler, S., 83
Wilson, B. R., 54, 66, 99
witch-hunt, 90